CONTENTS

PREFACE

by Nicolas de Oliveira, Nicola Oxley and Michael Petry

Installation, as a generic term, covers a large area of practice and enquiry within contemporary art. It is suggestive of the notion of 'exhibition', or 'display', and of an actual activity which is today as widespread as any other way of making art.

This book does not attempt to be all-inclusive, which would have been impossible given the very wide practice of installation. Nor does it seek to confine the subject by providing its ultimate definition. Rather it sets out a series of markers which outline the scale of its own task: to provide a focus on a highly complex practice.

Installation, as a hybrid discipline, is made up of multiple histories; it includes architecture and Performance Art in its parentage, and the many directions within contemporary visual arts have also exerted their influence. By crossing the frontiers between different disciplines, installation is able to question their individual autonomy, authority and, ultimately, their history and relevance to the contemporary context.

The prominence of installations in specific non-art sites also continues to figure among the concerns of installation artists. The activation of the place, or context, of artistic intervention suggests a localized, highly specific reading of the work, and is concerned not only with art and its boundaries, but with the continual rapprochement, or even fusion, of art and life. Installation must therefore also represent the artist's desire to extend the area of practice from the studio to the public space. By laying claim to territory beyond the private sphere, the artist is seen to widen the control that he/she has over the display of work.

Every book also contains a history of its own production, and *Installation Art* is no exception. It is underpinned by several years of research and extensive travel by the authors, and, necessarily, by a constant interaction with the practice. Discussions on the book began in 1989, at a time when the authors were responsible for the London-based Unit 7 Gallery, which was devoted to installation, and which, in turn, led to the establishment of the Museum of Installation.

We are indebted to Thames and Hudson for its support in bringing together this first book on the subject; to Michael Archer for his lucid texts; to Andrew Tullis for his research; to Edward Woodman for his archive of images, and to all those who have kindly lent photographic material, without whose help the book would not have been possible.

Because installation works may be created on one site and later recreated elsewhere, dates and titling can sometimes be variable. The same work, or a slightly altered work, may appear with different dates and titles.

FOREWORD

Installation, in the sense proposed by this book, is a relatively new term. It is really only in the last decade or so that it has been used to describe a kind of art making which rejects concentration on one object in favour of a consideration of the relationships between a number of elements or of the interaction between things and their contexts. In order to provide a structure for the book, the material has been placed in one of four sections: site, media, museum and architecture. These categories have no ultimate authority, and many artists make work which bears upon more than one of them. Similarly, they may also produce much else which could not be classified as installation at all. The sections, though, are more than arbitrary receptacles for the random allocation of material since their themes contribute to an understanding of what the term installation means. RoseLee Goldberg gave a 1975 article the title 'Space as Praxis' and it is this sense of space in active dialogue with the things and people it contains, in all its ramifications, that lies at the heart of the subject.[1] Procedures which activate the potential or repressed meanings of a specific place, which play real space and time off against the imaginative dimensions of the various electronic media, which question the cultural 'truths' reflected in patterns of collection, scholarship and display in the privileged spaces of art, and which relate the social space in which they operate to the sense of public, private and communal found in the language of architecture, all fall within the scope of the term.

Perhaps because installation is of such recent pedigree, it seems to enjoy a certain mobility of meaning. Yet there are galleries either wholly or partly devoted to it, from Amsterdam's De Appel in the early seventies through New York's PS1, Pittsburgh's Mattress Factory, London's Matt's Gallery to London's Museum of Installation in the late eighties. Coupled with the establishment of these smaller galleries, we have seen the appearance of a growing number of installations in the large group exhibitions of the international art circuit. The suggestively titled 'Ambiente' was staged as part of the Venice Biennale as long ago as 1976. More recently there have been the 1986 Chambres d'Amis project for which artists used rooms in private dwellings throughout Ghent, the 1987 Skulptur Projekte on sites around the town of Münster, and Berlin's Die Endlichkeit der Freiheit in 1990. The 1991 Carnegie International commissioned many of the selected artists to make installations within the framework of the Carnegie Museum's own collections and history, and the 1992 Documenta included a number of installations both within the various gallery spaces used for the show and outside, in the streets and parks of Kassel itself.

The idea that one could provide a history of installation is perhaps a curious one in view of its relative youth. Such a history can, however, be attempted although it must be more than a simple recounting of those occasions during the twentieth century on which similar forms have made an appearance. Of course, a list can easily be made: the inclusiveness of Futurism; Cubist collage; Duchamp's readymades; Dada and the constructions of Schwitters and Baader; El Lissitzky and Constructivist approaches to space; Duchamp again and his contributions to the Surrealist exhibitions in 1938 and 1942; Fontana's 'spatialism'; assemblage; Happenings; Klein and Manzoni; the Pop tableaux of Kienholz, Oldenburg, Segal and Thek; Fluxus; Minimalism; Land Art; Arte Povera; Process Art; Conceptualism; . . . But this is no more nor less than a history of modern art. What is needed, rather, is the drawing of certain ideas out of this history, particularly the notion that space and time (that is, actual duration rather than the abstract notion of time) themselves constitute material for art. We must also take note of the tendency, observable throughout modernism, for art to merge with life.

Marcel Duchamp, *Porte, 11, Rue Larrey*, 1927

TOWARDS INSTALLATION

Marcel Duchamp, *Bicycle Wheel*, 1951; third version after lost original of 1913

Does all this need an explanation? Is there any other explanation than the context of a world devoted to advertisements, overproduction, and horoscopes?
Marcel Broodthaers[1]

In *Les Peintres cubistes* (1913), Guillaume Apollinaire finished his consideration of Marcel Duchamp thus:

Just as Cimabue's pictures were paraded through the streets, our century has seen the airplane of Blériot, laden with the efforts humanity made for the past thousand years, escorted in glory to the [Academy of] Arts and Sciences. Perhaps it will be the task of an artist as detached from aesthetic preoccupations, and as intent on the energetic as Marcel Duchamp, to reconcile art and the people.[2]

Elitism versus populism, high versus low, avant-garde versus kitsch, individual creativity versus mass production – the distinction between the aesthetic space of art and the social space of the world around us has been drawn throughout this century with a variety of faces. In large part the history of modernism is a history of the impulse to establish some equivalence between these two arenas. Apollinaire's suspicions have proved well founded. Duchamp's readymades – mass-produced objects chosen for no good aesthetic reason and brought into the gallery as 'works of art' – challenged the basis upon which we distinguish the world of art from what lies outside it. The idea with *Bicycle Wheel*, the first readymade, was to spin it gently on entering the studio before going about one's business, so that it would flicker at the periphery of one's vision, 'like a fire in a grate'.[3] Fourteen years later, in 1927, Duchamp would again ruffle the domestic interior with his *Porte, 11, Rue Larrey*, a door hinged between two adjacent frames such that it would simultaneously be both closed and open. As with much art between 1960 and today, the period we might now refer to as postmodern, it is in coming to terms with the tendency exemplified in these gestures of Duchamp that installation has developed.

In the early 1960s the terms 'assemblage' and 'environment' were most commonly employed to describe work in which the artist had brought together a host of materials in order to fill a given space. At that time, installation referred to nothing more than how an exhibition had been hung. The essentially curatorial connotation is none the less still pertinent to our understanding of the active role played by space in contemporary installation. In his series of essays, *Inside the White Cube: The Ideology of the Gallery Space*, written in 1976, Brian O'Doherty (the New York-based Irish artist Patrick Ireland) discusses the fact that nowadays we have become highly aware of the attributes of the gallery itself when thinking about what it contains. Its walls and the volume of air bounded by them have assumed a significance which O'Doherty sees as dependent upon the two main strands of painterly development in the twentieth century: the exploration of the two-dimensional picture plane and the elaboration of the technique of collage. Collage interacts with the real space of the gallery by pulling material from the surrounding world and building it up on the painting's surface out into the spectator's viewing space.

With regard to our interest in the gallery's walls, O'Doherty mentions the Monet exhibition organized by William C. Seitz at the Museum of Modern Art in New York in 1960. For this show Seitz removed the canvases from their frames and in some cases even set them into the screens so that picture and support surface formed one continuous plane. Seitz's strategy was consonant with the investigation of the tension between the objective existence and the illusory function of paintings evident, for example, in the work of Frank Stella at that time. Stella discussed this in an interview with Bruce Glaser in 1964:

GLASER: Frank, your stretchers are thicker than usual. When your canvases are
        shaped or cut out in the center, this gives them a distinctly sculptural
        presence.

STELLA: I make the canvas deeper than ordinarily, but I began accidentally. I
        turned one-by-threes on edge to make a quick frame, and then I liked it.
        When you stand directly in front of the painting it gives it just enough
        depth to hold it off the wall; you're conscious of this sort of shadow, just
        enough depth to emphasize the surface. In other words, it makes it more
        like a painting and less like an object, by stressing the surface.[4]

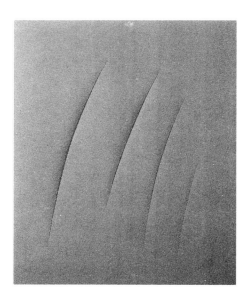

Lucio Fontana, *Spatial Concept (Attese)*, 1951

Compare this with Lucio Fontana's idea of *spazialismo* (spatialism), heralded in his *Manifesto blanco* (White manifesto) of 1946 and realized in his holed and slit canvases of the 1950s. Spatialism aimed at transcending the illusory space of traditional art works and integrating art with architecture and the larger environment. The holes and slashes attest to this aim by fracturing the coherence of the picture surface. Although he had moved away from the traditional rectangular format, Stella, in attempting to keep his works 'more like a painting and less like an object', is clearly not sharing Fontana's environmental concerns. The curatorial 'installation', however, brings these concerns into the equation willy-nilly. The image of Stella's shaped canvases, exhibited at the Leo Castelli Gallery in New York in the mid-sixties, is cited by O'Doherty as one example of a modernist *terminus*, since 'the colour field installation shot should be recognised as one of the teleological endpoints of the modern tradition'.[5] Also mentioned in this connection is William Anastasi's 1967 exhibition at the Dwan Gallery in New York, for which he produced silk-screened images of the walls of the gallery, slightly smaller than actual size, hanging the images on the appropriate surfaces. As O'Doherty wrote:

> Now a participant in, rather than a passive support for, the art, the wall became the locus of contending ideologies; and every new development had to come equipped with an attitude toward it.[6]

To the extent that the effort to render permeable that barrier which separates us – that is, the everyday world of mass-production – from the realm of the art work has succeeded, it has allowed meaning, the content of the work, to seep out into its surroundings. In breaking open the 'artistic realm' and making it one with social space, the observer of the work of art becomes implicated with it in a manner that differs considerably from the conventional relationship between viewer and painting or sculpture:

> As modernism gets older, context becomes content. In a peculiar reversal, the object introduced into the gallery 'frames' the gallery and its laws.[7]

The 'reversal' of which O'Doherty speaks here is a profound one since it affects not only the roles which work of art and gallery play in the drama of display, but also the way in which meaning arises out of the encounter between spectator and artwork. Meaning is no longer given, residing in the object until discerned by the perceptive viewer, it is something that is made in the encounter. The context that has taken on so much importance is as much as anything the entire cultural predisposition of the viewer. In a short article on Jim Dine written in 1963 – Dine had been involved in Happenings along with Allan Kaprow in the late 1950s and early 1960s before working in a Pop idiom – the Belgian artist Marcel Broodthaers quoted the curator and critic Pierre Schneider:

> The person who created this art – these paintings that make you laugh with scorn or that turn your stomach – the person whose only means of expression lie in choosing among the consumer goods someone else proposes to him – that person is you.[8]

The idea that the meaning of a work of art is not contained entirely within its frame or form is not, of course, a particularly new one. The roots of what today is called installation extend down through the mulch of modernism into the rich art historical loam beneath. Larger projects, such as chapels, houses or gardens, can be seen in numerous places as holding contexts for a variety of individual objects. What one must be cautious of, however, is taking formal similarity for conceptual precedent. To call some disposition of materials, objects or artefacts an installation with any degree of authority presupposes familiarity with a clutch of related terms: location, site, site-specificity, gallery, public, environment, space, time, duration. Consequently, a definition of installation must also shed light upon the contemporary significance of this surrounding vocabulary.

That formal congruence is not enough to guarantee an adequate definition is true even when we compare contemporary installation to that great, all-inclusive modernist notion of the *Gesamtkunstwerk*, the total work of art. Wagner's ideal of a creative synthesis which brought together poetry and music within the visual and dynamic framework of the operatic stage does have a place in the understanding of contemporary installation. As we shall see later, however, there are important conceptual differences between the *Gesamtkunstwerk* and installation today despite their having a common denominator in something which I, following the majority of commentators, shall call theatricality. The word is not ideal since it here refers not to the domain of drama proper, but to a consciousness of the processes of life and of one's part in them. An alternative would be to borrow from the linguistic theory of the Russian Mikhail Bakhtin the term 'carnival' which, in an essay on Bakhtin, the linguist and psychoanalyst Julia Kristeva defines thus:

> It is a spectacle, but without a stage; a game, but also a daily undertaking; a
> signifier, but also a signified. ... The scene of the carnival, where there is
> no stage, no 'theatre', is thus both stage and life, game and dream,
> discourse and spectacle.[9]

Installation is inclusive in a manner similar to the *Gesamtkunstwerk*, and a straightforward listing of its twentieth-century precedents would include aspects of Futurism, Dada, Constructivism and the Bauhaus programme, all of which, consciously or implicitly, owe something to it. But it is not until we stretch beyond Wagner's idea that installation's own parameters start to become clear.

A woodcut by Lyonel Feininger used as an emblem on the first proclamation of the Weimar Bauhaus in 1919 showed a Gothic cathedral. It was seen by the school's founder, Walter Gropius, as a symbol of the collaborative effort of a number of practitioners within a common architectural environment. Gropius spoke of imbuing creative work with an 'architectonic spirit', and in this wish to bring all aspects of art and craft together in the shared (and constructed) space of the community, he was consciously following on from Wagner's idea of the *Gesamtkunstwerk*.[10] Within the Bauhaus itself, Oskar Schlemmer developed this idea in his stage workshops. A return to basics led to the development

Lyonel Feininger, *Cathedral*
(Bauhaus Programme),1919

of scenarios employing nothing but changing forms, colours and lights. Schlemmer also worked on the idea of extending dramatic activity beyond the stage, that is, beyond the conceptual space/time framework within which the narrative exists:

> If we go so far as to break the narrow confines of the stage and extend the
> drama to include the building itself, not only the interior but the building
> as an architectural whole … we might demonstrate to a hitherto
> unknown extent the validity of the space-stage as an idea.[11]

In reaching back to the guild system of the Middle Ages for a social model that would encapsulate his own progressive ideas, Gropius had reproduced the double aspect of Wagner's original concept. *Gesamtkunst*, conceived as the re-establishment of Aeschylean tragedy in the spirit of nineteenth-century Germany, was an appeal to myth – in this case the idealized picture of civilization's roots in classical Greece – to underpin and sustain its forward-looking notion of a creative totality. Far from confining itself to the fine arts, this Janus-like quality was a central factor in the broader cultural life of the time. Walter Benjamin, for example, notes the mythic, fairytale (and finally hellish) element to the shopping arcades of Europe's major cities in his unfinished *Passagen-Werk* (Arcades Project) of the 1930s. 'The original temple of commodity capitalism', the arcades 'beamed out onto the Paris of the Second Empire like fairy grottoes.'[12] The ultimate expression of this wonderland of consumerism was the series of international fairs staged from 1851 onwards. In a note for the Project, Benjamin records Sigfried Giedion's comparison of these fairs to *Gesamtkunstwerke*.[13] We have, then, two versions of the spectacular: the collaboration between art forms and the mass culture of commodity capitalism. Installation becomes a possibility through the convergence of these two kinds of spectacle, or, at the very least, the laying of one over the other.

Totality of another kind can be seen in Futurism, and it offers two factors of importance. The first of these is Futurism's interest in realizing the potential in new materials and techniques, and the potential in applying new techniques to old media. In an Italian context we can perhaps see echoes of this in Fontana's encouragement of the use of such things as neon light and television in his pronouncements on Spatialism, and, subsequently, Mario Merz's own use of neon in his work. The second factor signalled by Futurism is the way in which the Futurist ideal itself was realized through such a variety of activities. In other words, it was not always the case that a pre-existent 'Futurist' notion could be applied to painting, sculpture, film, theatre, architecture, music, poetry and so on. Rather, the evidence of 'Futurist' endeavour across that range of disciplines, its very ubiquity, was to a certain degree constitutive of its meaning. A more up-to-date way of phrasing this would be to say that Futurism consisted in a series of principled 'interventions' into the various arts. This prefiguring of

F.T. Marinetti, *Words-in-Freedom*
(Irredentissimo), c. 1912

future developments in art, however, should not be taken too far. The language of F.T. Marinetti's 1909 'Founding and Manifesto of Futurism' is drenched in Symbolist imagery, and Futurist painting technique similarly owes much to late-nineteenth century theories of synaesthesia. Marinetti's *parole in libertà* (words in freedom), with their jumble of breathless description, advertising slogans, snatches of popular song and onomatopoeia, were attempts to express the confusion and interpenetration of sensory experiences. Similarly, in a painting such as Umberto Boccioni's *The Street Enters the House* (1911) we 'see' sounds and smells permeate the threshold between interior and exterior, and even the spaces themselves interfere visually with one another.

Artistic activity in Russia around the period of the Revolution maintained, for a short time, a fruitful tension between the 'pure' pursuit of art and the pressing demands of a society that would wish to see art's visual potential put to more directly communicative use. Vladimir Tatlin's *Monument to the Third International* was conceived in 1919 as 'a union of purely artistic forms (painting, sculpture and architecture) for a utilitarian purpose'.[14] Spiral in form and set at a dynamic diagonal, it was intended to house a cylindrical, a conical and a cubic work space, each of which was to revolve at a different rate. The last thing you were supposed to do in this building was to stand or sit; it was to be a monument to movement and the dynamism of the era. Prior to this Tatlin had been making Cubist-inspired constructions. The first of these were bas-relief collages with a background element, but this framing device was soon dispensed with so that the various parts of and the relationships within the relief could interact with the real space around it. In 1917, working with Alexander Rodchenko and Georgy Yakulov, Tatlin had devised the interior decorations for Moscow's Café Pittoresque, in which wood, metal and card constructions on walls and ceiling disturbed and fractured the solidity of the space.

Vladimir Tatlin, Model for a Monument to
the Third International, Moscow, 1919-20

Umberto Boccioni, *The Street Enters the House*, 1911

This attitude to the sculptural possibilities of space itself and of the passage of time was taken further in Constructivism by El Lissitzky, who hung his *Prouns* in Berlin's 1923 Russian exhibition in dynamic interrelationship with the galleries that contained them, and by Antoine Pevsner and Naum Gabo. In their 'Realistic Manifesto' of 1920 (written by Gabo and co-signed by his brother Pevsner) they proclaimed that: 'Space and time are the only forms on which life

El Lissitzky, Proun room, November Group's Art Exhibition, Berlin, 1923

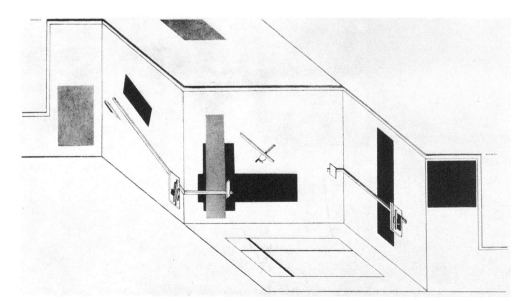

is built and hence art must be constructed.' 'Space and time', they said, 'are reborn to us today,'[15] a reference to the Futurists' first manifesto, written in 1909, in which Marinetti had said, 'Time and Space died yesterday.'[16] What had ceased to exist for Marinetti and his co-Futurists was the rational, ordered space that had hitherto existed within the frame of the art work. It was a space in which the relationships between things were clearly visible and in which cause and effect were comprehensible. The Futurists' image of a dynamic, fragmented, alogical world was essentially a theatrical one. Among the points made in a 1915 article, 'Futurist Synthetic Theatre', by Marinetti, Emilio Settimelli and Bruno Corra, is the following:

It's stupid to want to explain with logical minuteness everything entirely, in all its causes and consequences, because reality throbs around us, bombards us with *squalls of fragments of inter-connected events, mortised and tenoned together, confused, mixed up, chaotic.* E.g. it's stupid to act out a contest between two persons always in an orderly, clear, and logical way, since in daily life we nearly always encounter mere *flashes of argument* made *momentary* by our modern experience, in a tram, a café, a railway station, which remain cinematic in our minds like fragmentary dynamic symphonies of gestures, words, lights, and sounds.[17]

The Futurists, of course, even (or perhaps especially) saw war, 'the world's only hygiene', in the same theatrical terms. Marinetti's *Zang Tumb Tumb!* (1912) describes the sights and sounds of a battle with the Turks at Adrianopolis in terms of stage lighting and movement, and the noises of an orchestra. In fact, throughout the century it is the theatre that provides the arena for a metaphorical fusion of art and everyday life. Whether here, with the Futurists, at the Bauhaus in the 1920s (Oskar Schlemmer described painting as theoretical research and performance as the 'practice' of that classical equation between performer and space), in the blocked out and scripted Happenings of Allan Kaprow, Jim Dine and others in the late 1950s, or in the raw confrontation between viewer and Minimal sculpture (a confrontation described by the critic Michael Fried in 1967 as essentially theatrical), it is the space and time of the theatrical experience which pass for the extensiveness of quotidian existence.

The aspects of Kurt Schwitters's activities which might now be called installations also have a theatrical pedigree. His *Merzbau*, constructed in a number of rooms in his Hanover house throughout the 1920s and up until he left Germany in 1936, was begun after Schwitters's first elaboration of his idea for a *Merzbühne*, a Merz theatre. This was from the outset recognized as a project for the realization of a *Gesamtkunstwerk*.[18] Schwitters made the *Merzsäule* (Merz Column), the first element of what was to become the *Merzbau*, in 1919. In some respects it resembled Johannes Baader's *Das Grosse Plasto-Dio-Dada-Drama 'Deutschlands Grosse und Untergang'* (The Great Plastic

Dio-Dada-Drama 'Germany's Greatness and Downfall'), the six-storey collaged structure built for the 1920 Berlin Dada Fair, although the revolutionary political intent behind Baader's work differed from Schwitters's requirement that the *Merzbau* function as some form of container for a variety of objects which bore commemorative and autobiographical significance. Starting as a Dada-inspired work, the *Merzbau* took on a more consciously Constructivist look during the twenties.

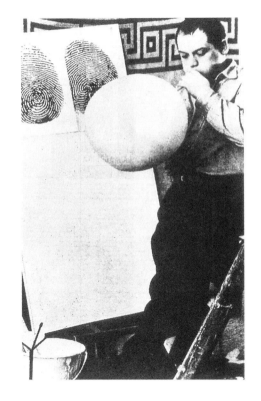

This laying over of Dadaist beginnings and the approach in general to the making of what was, to begin with at least, a very private work (Schwitters, a great self-publicist, did not admit to its existence in print until 1931), marks Schwitters as an important reference point for any consideration of the contribution which Joseph Beuys's work made to the concept of installation from the 1960s onwards. Beuys is an interesting figure since his undoubted importance in this field is not the result of his forcing a simple break with the techniques and strategies of high modernist art. Involved in performances and actions with Fluxus during the sixties, instrumental in setting up the German Green Party whose radical approach to the environment is echoed in much that now goes under the rubric of Land Art, consistent producer of works demonstrating enormous material inventiveness which can only be described as installations, he nevertheless looks backwards as much as forwards. The appearance of installation is but one expression of the gradual detachment in postmodern culture of meaning from things. For Beuys, however, this disconnection is not a particularly significant one. In his 1980 article bearing the mock-Wagnerian title 'Beuys: The Twilight of the Idol', Benjamin Buchloh contrasted Beuys's response to Duchamp with that of his European contemporaries:

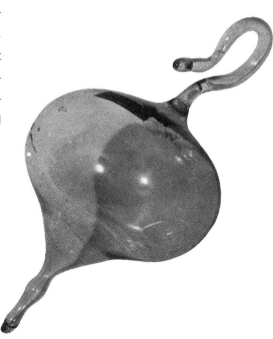

> Unlike his European peers from the late 1950s – Piero Manzoni, Arman or even Yves Klein – Beuys does not change the *state of the object within the discourse* itself. Quite to the contrary, he dilutes and dissolves the conceptual precision of Duchamp's readymade by reintegrating the object into the most traditional and naive context of representation of meaning, the idealist metaphor: this object stands for that idea, and that idea is represented in this object.[19]

Above **Marcel Duchamp,** *Air de Paris***, 1919**

Top **Piero Manzoni making** *The Artist's Breath***, 1961**

Klein's showmanship – for example, *Le Vide*, his 1958 exhibition of the entirely empty Iris Clert gallery – and Manzoni's celebration of the artist's person contributed to a shift in our acceptance of what constituted the art object. Klein's unremarkable paintings become interesting as evidence of their bravura production: canvases burnt with a blow torch, or surfaces smeared, under his direction, by paint-soaked nude models. Duchamp's *Air de Paris* (1919), bottled as a present to his collectors the Arensbergs, is transformed by Manzoni into *The Artist's Breath* (1961), an inflated balloon which quickly became, and remains, a shrivelled reminder of its former 'inspiration'. Arman

First public exhibition of
Yves Klein's *Anthropometries of
the Blue Period*, 9 March 1960

Daniel Spoerri, *Dinner by Dorothy Prodber*,
1964

began his *Poubelles*, rubbish from a waste bin displayed in a glass box, in 1960. In the same year, too, he 'replied' to Klein's *Le Vide* with his own show at Iris Clert: two truckloads of rubbish dumped in the gallery, entitled *Le Plein*. At around the same time Daniel Spoerri started producing *tableaux pièges* (snare pictures), wall-mounted tables whose tops were covered with an assemblage of meal leftovers. The work of all these artists began to question precisely what it is we are required to focus on when looking at art. Are these things important in themselves, or meaningful as a sediment left from some previous turbulence? But Beuys's ambivalence towards Duchamp is by no means the whole story:

In other cases ... there simply can be no doubt about Beuys' original vision in introducing into a sculptural discourse issues that became crucial years later in Minimal and post-Minimal art. If we compare Beuys' *Fat Corner* (1960?), with Richard Serra's *Splash Piece* (1968), we discover a comparable concern for the dissolution of a traditional object/construct-oriented conception of sculpture in favour of a more process-bound and architectural understanding of sculptural production and perception.[20]

Donald Judd, Four untitled works of 1991, installed at the Pace Gallery, New York

North American art of the decade between the mid-sixties and mid-seventies, the Minimalism and post-Minimalism to which Buchloh refers in the quote above, offers much to an understanding of installation. Donald Judd, writing a survey of the year's exhibitions in New York in 1965, introduced his notion of the 'specific object'.[21] The specific object differed from traditional art works in that it was a simple, unified form rather than a whole constituted from the coherent relationship of internal parts. Thinking along the same lines in his 'Notes on Sculpture' (1966), Robert Morris stressed the importance of 'simpler forms that create strong gestalt sensations'.[22] What was also new about what we now call Minimalism was the refusal of its objects to sit comfortably within either of the accepted categories of painting or sculpture. As an alternative, Judd termed it 'three-dimensional work', a phrase which not only suggested how close to sculpture it was, but also emphasized how similar it was to any other kind of (non-art) object.

Morris's 'Notes' describe how the absence of differentiation within such objects 'takes relationships out of the work and makes them a function of space, light, and the viewer's field of vision'. The 'self-reflexive' experiencing of such work 'necessarily exists in time', something which is quite different from Cubism's 'concern for simultaneous views in one plane'. We are dealing now not with a straightforward meeting of viewer and artwork in the idealized atmosphere of the gallery, but of an experience within a 'complex and expanded field'. Morris raises 'an obvious question' which, as it were, acknowledges the inevitability of the Land Art which was to appear in subsequent years:

Robert Morris, *Observatory*, 1971.
Santpoort-Velsen, The Netherlands

Why not put the work outside and further change the terms? A real need exists
to allow this next step to become practical. Architecturally designed
sculpture courts are not the answer nor is the placement of work outside
cubic architectural forms. Ideally, it is a space without architecture as background and reference, that would give different terms to work with.[23]

In spite of Morris's identification of the increasingly significant part
played by the artwork's context, however, he was still thinking in terms of
an encounter between spectator and object:

That the space of the room becomes of such importance does not mean that an
environmental situation is being established.[24]

The late 1960s in the United States saw an interesting set of responses
to Minimalism's clean-cut objects. Artists like Richard Serra, Bruce Nauman,
Eva Hesse, Lynda Benglis and Barry Le Va produced work whose look was
intricately bound up with the series of procedures which brought it into
being. For example, one of Barry Le Va's 'distributed sculptures' of 1966, a
floor arrangement of coloured felt and ball-bearings, has the title *Bought,
Cut, Placed, Folded, Dropped, Thrown (Green, Purple, Blue, Red)*.[25] Much of
this sculpture also, in contrast to Minimalism's formal clarity, appeared loosely
structured and diffuse, seeming at times to reject altogether the idea that its
material constituted an object. Now, in addition to an unease with the

traditional categories of painting and sculpture, there was added confusion over just what it was that one was supposed to be looking at. Max Kozloff voiced his bewilderment in an exhibition review at the time:

After all, we are not accustomed to stepping on sculpture which appears to be some kind of leaving. Nor do we expect it to seem merely a sullying and spotting of the surfaces which enclose us.[26]

Allan Kaprow, *Yard* (Happening), 1961

Writing in *Artforum* of this new kind of work in 1968, Robert Morris said: 'Disengagement with preconceived enduring forms and orders for things is positive assertion. It is part of the work's refusal to continue estheticizing form by dealing with it as a prescribed end.'[27] That essay was titled 'Anti-Form' by the editors at *Artforum*, and that term along with Process Art became a common tag for post-Minimal sculpture.

Both Kozloff – in his review quoted above of '9 at Castelli', the show selected by Morris that first brought this work to wider notice – and Morris himself – in 'Anti-Form' – link the dispersal of materials around the gallery space in Process Art back to the gestural freedoms of Abstract Expressionist painting.[28] In the same vein, Robert Pincus-Witten suggested that post-Minimal sculpture 'sponsors the sensibilities covered by [Heinrich] Wölfflin's term *malerisch*'.[29] But quite apart from a formal looseness that echoes painterly expressiveness, there is another, perhaps more significant relationship between Process Art and Abstract Expressionism which comes out in the characterization of the earlier movement as, in Harold Rosenberg's words, 'action painting':

At a certain moment the canvas began to appear to one American painter after another as an arena in which to act – rather than as a space in which to reproduce, re-design, analyze or 'express' an object, actual or imagined. What was to go on the canvas was not a picture but an event.[30]

Claes Oldenburg, *The Store*, 1965

Rosenberg's early-1950s argument, shaped in response to the emphasis Jackson Pollock placed on the act of painting, looks forward to the later vocabulary of environments, happenings, actions and events. Allan Kaprow, speaking of his gallery environments, made the connection explicit, stating that his 'action-collage technique' derived from an interest in Pollock. Kaprow's early environments filled the available space with works, works-in-progress and other material, but dissatisfaction with the contrived necessity that they end at the gallery wall led him to move beyond the gallery and work outside. George Segal and Claes Oldenburg were also involved in early Happenings, Segal then going on to exhibit his tableaux including figures modelled from the human body, and Oldenburg to make his *Store* installation and *Store Days* performances. There were, too, Jim Dine's 1960 *Car Crash* performance, Ed Kienholz's tableaux from 1959, and the wrappings of Christo which began in 1958.

From Jim Dine, *Car Crash*, 1960

Robert Rauschenberg, *Charlene*, 1954

Jannis Kounellis, *Cavalli* (Horses), 1969-76

In relation to this activity. it is worth noting the shift which Robert Rauschenberg made in the early sixties from his 'combine' painting/assemblages to canvases which contained multiple silk-screened images drawn from the media and from the history of art. It was in talking of these works that the critic Leo Steinberg made one of the earliest uses of the term 'postmodern'. Likening them to 'flatbeds', that is, printing frames, he suggested that they alter the traditional relationship between spectator and art object, which had remained even in Cubist collage, because of the heterogeneity and logical incompatibility of their various elements. The kind of perception they demand is much more akin to the manner in which we address culture at large. [31]

What gains were there from post-Minimal developments in sculpture? Kozloff wrote:

As a reaction to the rigid, minimal sculpture that immediately preceded it, it displays much of the same conceptual coolness and devaluation of 'relationships' at the same time that it opens up new possibilities of freedom from the object and collaboration with the environment.[32]

The features Kozloff remarks upon here accord with the characteristics which, in the same year (1968), the Italian critic Germano Celant was finding in the work of Jannis Kounellis, Giuseppe Penone, Giovanni Anselmo, Mario Merz, Michelangelo Pistoletto and others. Celant termed this work Arte Povera (poor art), not because it was made from inexpensive materials, but because it was empty of specific content. Art which is not about anything can offer no meaning. What it can offer is information of varying kinds, and it is this

Michelangelo Pistoletto, *Venus degli Stracci* (Venus of the Rags), 1967

information circulating in the open field of social relations that in its turn generates possible meanings.

Kozloff's 'devaluation of relationships', however, was already something with a fair history. The event that is recognized as the first 'Happening' had taken place at Black Mountain College, North Carolina, in 1952. Conceived by John Cage, it involved a number of participants – artists, musicians, poets, dancers – simply, in Cage's words, 'doing what they do' in front of an audience spread among four differently oriented blocks of seats. During his period of study under Arnold Schoenberg, Cage had finally rejected the conventional and, in traditional musical terms, indispensable idea of composition; that is, the internal relation of parts within a coherent musical whole. In its place he practised music-making, and subsequently writing and installation, as a process more akin to the chance encounters and stimuli that impinge upon us in everyday life. His introduction to Zen Buddhism led to use of the *I Ching* as a means of 'composing' by choosing randomly from among a set of possible options, an aleatory procedure which carried forward Duchamp's use of chance operations.

The various contributions to the 1952 Happening were not co-ordinated, and the members of the audience, who, because of the arrangement of the chairs would see and hear different things according to where they sat, were left to construct their own path through the varied elements bombarding them. At the end of the performance, the plastic cup that had been placed on each chair at the outset was filled with coffee regardless of what the seat's occupant had done to it in the interim. The demands placed upon the audience by this event are central to an understanding of installation. It is they who, in a very real sense, are left to construct the meaning of what is going on before them. This meaning cannot be read off or recognized because it, insofar as 'it' implies a preconceived, unitary idea that the protagonists are attempting to impart, does not exist. Karlheinz Stockhausen's description of Cage as 'a composer who draws attention to himself more by his actions than by his productions', is apposite.[33] Fundamentally, we are dealing with a shift from art as object to art as process, from art as a 'thing' to be addressed, to art as something which occurs in the encounter between the onlooker and a set of stimuli. In this regard the nomenclature is appropriate in that a 'Happening' of this kind offers itself as a model for events in the everyday which really do (just) happen.

Roughly contemporary with the development of Happenings in the U.S., Europe witnessed the forming of the Situationist International in 1957. Along with Guy Debord, the movement's chief ideologue and moving spirit, a key early figure was the painter Asger Jorn, who had previously been part of the CoBrA group of post-Surrealist painters. The first issue of the journal, *Internationale Situationiste*, published in 1958, contained a list of definitions. Some of the terms on this list bear significantly on the development of an aesthetic view that sees art in the context of everyday life rather than as operating in a realm distinct from it. There is the idea of a 'situation' itself, 'a moment of life concretely and deliberately constructed by the collective organization of a unitary ambiance and a game of events'.[34] The growing sense that the viewer was important, and that art's meaning was actively produced in its reception or consumption as much as its production, is inherent in the idea of 'psychogeography', 'the study of the specific effects of the geographical environment, consciously organized or not, on the emotions and behaviour of individuals'. Related to psychogeography is the term '*dérive*', or 'drift', used to describe one's passage through a number of different ambiences (that is, through the modern urban environment) in an endeavour to observe their effect upon the person. Quite clearly, *dérive* owes much to the enigmatic person observed in Edgar Allan Poe's short story, 'The Man in the Crowd', who wanders calmly in busy thoroughfares but with increasing agitation in less heavily populated side roads, and to Baudelaire's figure of the *flâneur*, a disinterested yet engaged observer of all around him.

Relevant, too, to the parameters defining contemporary installation is the notion of '*détournement*', the appropriation of previously existing aesthetic artefacts in order to divert their meaning or intent. To this end it was asserted that 'there can be no situationist painting or music, but only a situationist use of these means'. Debord rejected any idea that art could exist within a realm distinct from that of political revolutionary activity. (It was his insistence on this point that led to Jorn's early departure from what was at the best of times a highly fissiparous group.) Ironically though, as the critic Peter Wollen pointed out in 1989, Situationism's success in the unrest of 1968 was a cultural rather than a political one. The theories propounded in Debord's 1967 book, *The Society of the Spectacle*, were 'more or less reduced to the title of his book, generalized as an isolated catch phrase'.[35]

It was in 1967 that Michael Fried wrote 'Art and Objecthood', his noted essay on Minimalism (Fried used the term 'literalism'). What Morris had characterized in his 'Notes on Sculpture' as an encounter between viewer and sculpture, Fried saw as a confrontation. Although it looked more like sculpture, Judd saw 'three-dimensional work' as being closer to painting since, for him, painting's progress in the twentieth century had been towards a realization of its own objecthood.[36] This is precisely the problem discussed by Stella in his interview with Glaser quoted earlier. Fried, critical of Minimalism, looked for objecthood's defeat in 'shape', and for the instantaneous manifestation of a work in all its aspects so that it might overcome the duration required for its unfolding. Experiencing Minimal art was, for Fried, an instance of 'theatre': meaning unfolded as a consequence of the spectator's awareness of his or her relationship, psychological, physical and imaginative, to the object. From this point on, the inherent relativity of the viewing experience itself became one of the most crucial factors for artists to explore.

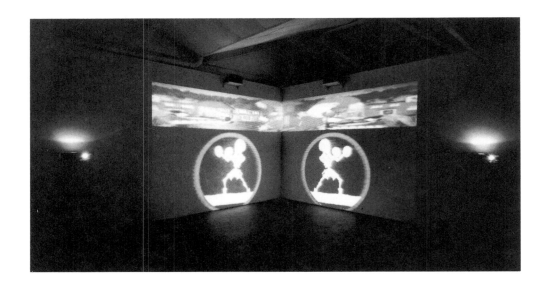

What is being charted here – the fracturing of the artwork and the dispersal of its meanings across the cultural field – has its corollary in a challenge to the simple integrity of the viewing subject mounted by feminism. Far from being an anonymous or universal cipher, the spectator is sexed and the possessor of a personal cultural history which predisposes him or her to view things in the light of certain interests or assumptions. Since the later sixties, the introduction into the making of and thinking about art of conceptual models drawn in particular from psychoanalysis has led to the development of an understanding that the spectator's position in relation to a work of art is not a fixed 'point of view', but is itself the continually transforming upshot of the processes and conflicting impulses of the social experience. Exemplary in this respect are Mary Kelly's extended work, *Post-Partum Document*, which examines the relationship between the artist and her son during the first five years of his life, and Susan Hiller's installations such as *Fragments*, *Belshazzar's Feast* and *An Entertainment*, which draw in their structuring on her earlier training in anthropology.

The implication of Minimalism, not initially embraced by Morris but there none the less, was that one could no longer straightforwardly perceive art as being somehow manifest in the objects before one. These things took on more the role of a trigger, an excuse to engage or indulge in the experience of art. The art historian Lucy Lippard has famously termed this falling away of embodied or inherent authority as 'the dematerialization of the art object'.[37] This is not to say that things literally underwent a process of physical attenuation, although in some late-1960s and early-1970s Conceptualism that was true too. It is more that what we had hitherto thought of as 'works of art' functioned now as what the American cultural theorist Fredric Jameson recently called 'material occasions for the viewing process'.[38] Jameson has written at length on the particular kind of spatial experience that characterizes postmodernism, and for him this new mode of address is an aspect of that 'spatialization':

Or, to put it more punchily, the gallery has ceased its conventional activity of showing objects and become 'a place to experience experience'.[40] Fried saw the incursion of theatre into art as an unwelcome development. Evaluation of its desirability aside, however, it has undoubtedly been one of the indispensable critical concepts in the years since then. In terms of the subject under discussion here, what Fried's essay does is to recognize the limited relevance of the concept of *Gesamtkunstwerk*. The totality to which not only Wagner, but also Gropius, the Constructivists, even Schwitters aspired, was one wrought from the coming together of quite distinct areas of creativity. Fried's assertion that 'art degenerates as it approaches the condition of theatre' (which he illustrates by bracketing the 'theatrical' Cage and Rauschenberg together as against, respectively, Elliot Carter and Morris Louis), was an attempt to reject as unpalatable the realization that the certainties and norms of the various art forms had been destabilized. By the late 1980s Jameson could accept the fact of such destabilization as a prerequisite for any discussion of meaning in an installation in which Robert Gober had included not only his own work, but also that of his peers Meg Webster and Richard Prince, and of the nineteenth-century painter Alfred Bierstadt:

As the New York artist and critic John Miller has pointed out, Fried's concept of 'theatre' 'succeeds . . . in clarifying the relationship between Minimalist sculpture and outright commodities. Friedian theatre in this way dovetails with Guy Debord's concept of the spectacle. By articulating something of Minimalism's unintentioned significations, Fried went beyond its stated

Robert Smithson, installation view from the Entropic Landscape exhibition, IVAM, Valencia, 1993

agenda to identify tendencies which continue to influence, if not dominate, art production to this day.'[42] Inexorably, art's skirmishing with a sense of theatre – and theatre, according to Cage, 'is what we're really living in'[43] – drags it out of its own ideal realm into that larger 'dream world' of commodity capitalism which Walter Benjamin explored in his *Passagen Werk*. The contemporary shopping mall, epitome of Jameson's postmodern 'spatialization', finds its predecessor in the nineteenth-century arcades of Europe's capital cities. And just as for Benjamin the need was to wake up from this dream to the realities of capitalism, so a major aspect of the 1960s' radicalization of space and of the body in space which led to the development of installation and performance was the wish to address economic and political realities through an unsettling of the certainties of the art world.

Gordon Matta-Clark, *Conical Intersect*, 1975

Since then, the widespread adoption of installation as a method of art production has led to a situation in which it is fast coming to seem the conventional way to do things. In the section introductions which follow, therefore, it is necessary to consider the theoretical contributions which a number of artists have made to the varied aspects of contemporary installation. Through both his work and writings, Robert Smithson did much to crystallize the central concept of 'site' and to provide a way of thinking about the relationship between the space of the gallery and the surrounding environment; Fluxus artists such as Nam June Paik seized upon the newly available technology of mass communication in order to investigate its possibilities; Marcel Broodthaers, in continuing on from and subverting Duchamp's radicalism, provided a critique of the museum which was at once powerful and amusing; and Gordon Matta-Clark, by cutting into the physical fabric of buildings, gave concrete expression to issues of community and urban life which a number of artists have subsequently explored through an engagement with architecture.

Right **Marcel Broodthaers,** *La Salle Blanche,* **1975**

SITE

During the sixties, the idea of an artwork as 'environment' was elaborated beyond the basic fact that the spectator should, rather than looking at it, inhabit it as he or she inhabits the world. A key figure in this development was Robert Smithson, who formulated the distinction between a Site, a particular place or location in the world at large, and a Nonsite, a representation in the gallery of that place in the form of transported material, photographs, maps and related documentation. It was important to make this distinction because while Smithson and other American land artists such as Michael Heizer, Nancy Holt, James Turrell and Walter de Maria were operating in places other than galleries, their work remained dependent upon the interpretative framework provided by the gallery system. This was true also of the very different land-based activities of British artists Richard Long and Hamish Fulton. Holt encapsulated her awareness of this interdependence in an 'I wish' statement in 1980:

Ideally, I would like to live six months a year at my sculpture sites, and six months in New York, where I can work on videotapes, films, photography and drawings.[1]

Smithson listed ten points of difference between Sites and Nonsites:

	SITE	NONSITE
1	Open limits	Closed limits
2	A series of points	An array of matter
3	Outer coordinates	Inner coordinates
4	Subtraction	Addition
5	Indeterminate certainty	Determinate uncertainty
6	Scattered information	Contained information
7	Reflection	Mirror
8	Edge	Centre
9	Some place (physical)	No place (abstraction)
10	Many	One[2]

Implicit in both Smithson's terminology and his enumeration of the relevant polarities is the idea that a work, rather than merely occupying a designated place, actually constitutes that place.

The irreducible complex of work, place, and the experience of both over time by the spectator comes out clearly from Walter de Maria's notes for his *Lightning Field* (1977). Set in a semi-arid plateau in New Mexico, the work comprises vertical steel poles spaced out within a 1 mile by 1 kilometre grid. The length of the poles varies with the terrain so that their tips form a single plane which 'would evenly support an imaginary sheet of glass'. Scattered among de Maria's careful, almost obsessive accounting of the brute facts of this huge work (like much American Land Art of the late sixties and seventies it is a true 'installation' in the more conventional sense of the word), we find such statements as:

The land is not the setting for the work but a part of the work.

A simple walk around the perimeter of the poles takes approximately two hours.

Because the sky–ground relationship is central to the work, viewing The Lightning Field from the air is of no value.

And

It is intended that the work be viewed alone, or in the company of a very small number of people, over at least a 24-hour period.[3]

For Regina Cornwell the imaginary sheet of glass suggests a balancing act between art and nature, and between the small audience and large landscape. It also intimates a desire to return art to life, although in order to do so *The Lightning Field* paradoxically calls for isolation.[4] Cornwell's suggestion is reinforced by the fact that the idea of the glass sheet coupled with the tone of de Maria's notes is reminiscent of Duchamp's *(To Be Looked At [From The Other Side Of The Glass] With One Eye, Close To, For Almost An Hour)* (1918).

Smithson spoke of his interest in the 'site' as a desire to 'return to the origins of material'. What the spectator encountered in the gallery – a sculpture or a painting – was 'refined matter'.[5] The challenge, then, was to make a kind of journey, following things back to their original state. In making the move we are going back in time as much as travelling elsewhere in space. Smithson's 'site' is thus a place not only of environmental, but also of historical and even archaeological interest. As such it presents both the stuff of the world and our attempts to grasp and comprehend it intellectually as inextricably bound up with one another. This is a much richer idea than a simple reading of nature as an uncomplicated 'other' to culture or urban life, since here, 'getting away' from the sophisticated space of the gallery into the world at large, whether in an urban or a non-urban setting, means getting back to the root forms of perception and comprehension. In works like *Partially Buried Woodshed*, in which earth was piled around and on top of an old shed until its support beams collapsed, and the *Texas Overflow* project, in which asphalt would be pumped into a heaped-up basin of limestone rocks until it spilled over, Smithson found concrete metaphors for the kind of mental deliberations demanded by a fragmented world. The aesthetic experience is somehow forged out of the struggle to impose structure upon an environment subject to entropic forces:

One's mind and the earth are in constant erosion, mental rivers wear away abstract banks, brain waves
undermine cliffs of thought, ideas decompose into stones of unknowing, and conceptual
crystallizations break apart into deposits of gritty reason. Vast moving faculties occur in this
geologic miasma, and they move it the most physical way. This movement seems motionless, yet
it crushes the landscape of logic under glacial reveries. This slow flowage makes one conscious
of the turbidity of thinking. Slump, debris slides, avalanches all take place within the cracking
limits of the brain. The entire body is pulled into the cerebral sediment, when particles and
fragments make themselves known as solid consciousness. A bleached and fragmented world
surrounds the artist. To organize this mess of corrosion into patterns, grids, and subdivisions is
an esthetic process that has scarcely been touched.[6]

Nowadays, artists find it possible to use the gallery itself as a site. Guillaume Bijl turns art spaces into a used car showroom, a gymnasium or a menswear store, Joseph Kosuth uses them to deliberate upon the complexities of representation in our culture, Ilya Kabakov remodels them as, for example, residential apartments or an abandoned school, while Christian Boltanski transforms them into archives. For some, then, the gallery as a *type* of space can be seen as a more or less anonymous cultural site that is the most appropriate place in which to install art. Vito Acconci is one who chose to 'use the gallery as the place where the "art" actually occurred' instead of 'as a sign … for work that was really occurring elsewhere'.

By making [that] choice, then, I was shifting my concentration from 'art-doing' to 'art-experiencing':
an artwork would be done specifically for a gallery – in other words for a peopled space, for a
space in which there were gallery-goers. The gallery, then, could be thought of as a community
meeting place, a place where a community could be formed, where a community could be called
to order, called to a particular purpose.[7]

On the other hand, an enlargement upon the idea of the site can be seen in the growing use of the related term, 'site-specific', over the past decade. Site-specificity implies neither simply that a work is to be found in a particular place, nor, quite, that it is that place. It means, rather, that what the work looks like and what it means is dependent in large part on the configuration of the space in which it is realized. In other words, if the same objects were arranged in the same way in another location, they would constitute a different work. Richard Serra's work, and, in a different way, that of Maria Nordman, has developed this notion. What is important about a space can be any one of a number of things: its dimensions (Serra, Richard Venlet), its general character, the materials from which it is constructed, the use to which it has previously been put (Anya Gallaccio), the part it played in an event of historical or political significance, and so on. These are factors which, to a greater or lesser extent, have relevance for all the sections in this book.

CHRISTO has completed many ambitious projects, including wrapping buildings, surrounding islands with floating plastic skirts and fencing in miles of coastline and inland hills. All these have taken years of patience and planning. The sale of the preparatory drawings funds the works. In fact, drawings and collages add to the development of the ideas and serve as a pre-document to compare with the actuality.

Since all Christo's projects are site specific and time based (they are often up for only a few days or weeks), they can be looked upon as large-scale site installations. The whole process is part of the work, be it committee meetings with town planners, court hearings to overrule bureaucratic roadblocks, the installation of the work, or its removal.

One of his most recent projects, *The Umbrellas Japan – USA 1984-91*, linked the two countries by a series of massive blue and yellow umbrellas. The umbrellas opened and closed and stood 6 metres high, with a diameter of almost 9 metres.

▲ The drawing above is from 1988 and shows blue umbrellas sited along the Satokawa River in Japan. The photograph right shows the same site in 1991. The Japanese site, in Ibaraki, 72 miles north of Tokyo, and the Californian site, 60 miles north of Los Angeles, are located in similar valley formations. The work was completed in October 1991.

The Mexican artist Orozco and the Spanish artist Perejaume intervene on both natural and manmade environments.

▲ **GABRIEL OROZCO**'s interventions are small and poetic. In *Planets in the Volcano* (1992) at the Popocatepetl Volcano in Mexico (above), he placed snowballs on two already existing lines of wooden posts.

➤ **PEREJAUME**'s installation *Cim del Catiu d'Or* (opposite) of 1988, consisted of a thick, gilt, custom-made frame which followed the natural geological contours of a virtually arbitrary natural space.

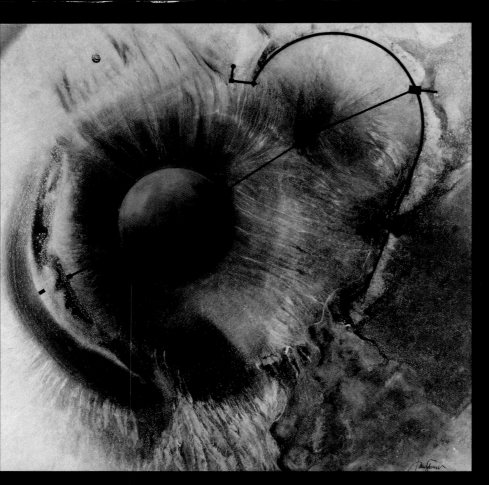

The U.S. artist **JAMES TURRELL** conceived his *Roden Crater* project in 1972, eventually purchasing the crater and surrounding land near Flagstaff, Arizona, in 1977. He carved concrete chambers into the site to allow views of the sky. Turrell's 1985 plan, 'Finished Crater Topographical', is shown below left; 'Basic Floor Plans' (1991) is shown left. When the project is completed the site will contain a museum, library, planetarium, airport and visitor centre.

Razor (opposite above) **is representative of Turrell's works for the gallery space. He has stated that his interest is in 'the perception of space and how light inhabits space' and in this piece, shown at the Anthony d'Offay Gallery, London, in 1991, he used artificial and natural light to create a room of pure blue space. The light from outside the gallery mediated the artificial light inside. In** *Rondo* (opposite below) **Turrell created another visually deceptive environment, again through the use of light. The work is dated 1968-69 and is now in the Newport Harbor Art Museum, California.**

An exploration of the physical nature of a site can reveal its fragile archaeology and its aesthetic resonance for the viewer. Large or small interventions can have a significant impact on how we view the site.

◄ Left **SHELAGH WAKELY**'s *Curcuma sul Travertino* (1991) was sited in the entrance hall of the British School at Rome, in the Borghese Gardens. A thin layer of turmeric spice covered the richly patterned travertine marble floor. The movement of visitors gradually erased the patterning on the spice itself, which eventually disappeared. The work lasted for only one week.

▲ Above In **KATHY PRENDERGAST**'s untitled 1987 installation at Unit 7 Gallery, London, the floor was covered with carved pieces of white chalk-stone. The dust from the carving was sieved through two mesh objects, the larger (seen here) resembled a cone and hung from the rafters; the other, a pair of hands, was mounted on the back wall. On a side wall hung a large charcoal drawing of the stones.

➤ Opposite **EVE ANDREE LARAMEE**'s *The Eroded Terrain of Memory* (1990) at Wesleyan University Gallery, Middletown, Connecticut, was based on the geological history of the building's limestone walls, and the university's siting between two major geological faults. The work took the form of a suspended glass faultline – made of mobile glass plates, steel wire and a ton of mica, quartz and feldspar – and a landslide consisting of an inclined wall

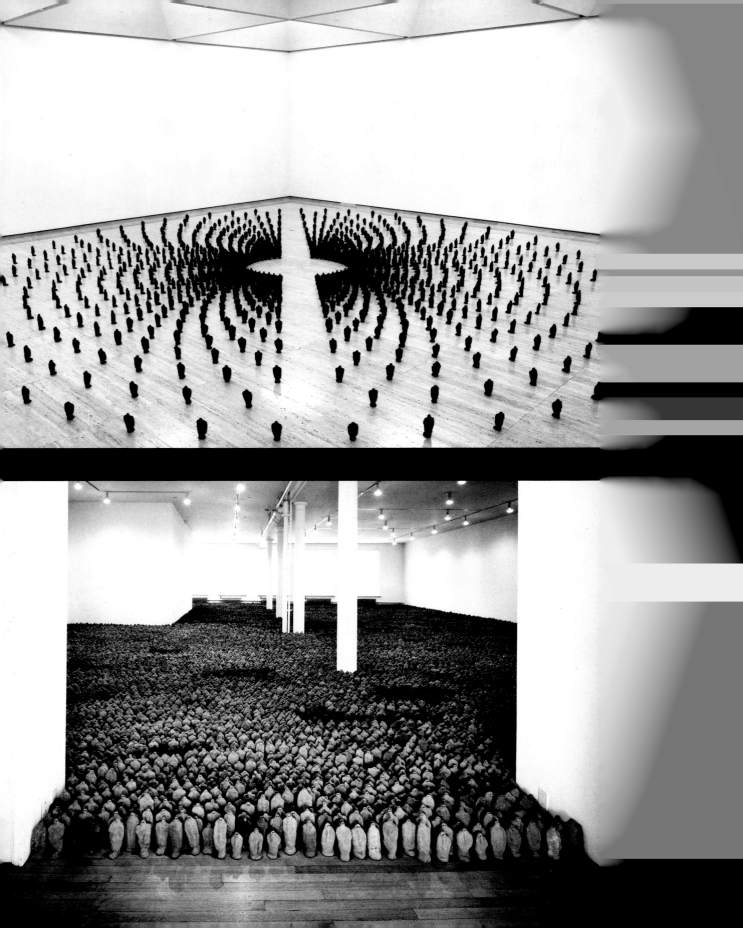

▲ The British artist **RICHARD LONG** works primarily with natural materials. In 1987 he created *Stonefield* (above) at the Allotment, Renshaw Hall, Liverpool, for the Coracle Atlantic Foundation. Until 1985, the building had served as the city's unemployment office (top). At the time of Long's installation, Coracle had cleared the site of its fittings and was renovating the building to serve as an alternative art space, prior to the completion of the Liverpool Tate. Long created a massive rectangle (37 x 20 metres) of white limestone chippings. He contributed to the Foundation by paying for the stone and for the additional workers needed to complete the installation. Although the project was a success, the city revoked Coracle's licence soon after. The building remains empty.

◀ In **ULRICH RUCKRIEM**'s intervention in the ruins of the nave of Kirkstall Abbey, Leeds, in 1993 (opposite), **six triangular green dolomite slabs echoed the original columns of the abbey.**

➤ **GIUSEPPE PENONE** installed *Pages de terre – I et II* (Pages of Earth – I and II) and *Ho intrecciato fra lore tre alberelli* (I Have Entwined between Their Three Trees) **at the Durand-Dessert Gallery, Paris, in 1987** (right). **It comprises three works from 1968 to 1985: two** *Pages de terre* **were placed around** *Ho intrecciato*. **Thick pieces of terracotta were placed on top of branches and on hoes and pickaxes. A gnarled tree trunk separated the** *Pages*.

La Rencontre de 2 oeuvres (Meeting of 2 Works) **by GIOVANNI
➤ ANSELMO** (right) **was shown at the Durand-Dessert Gallery, Paris, in 1990. Five thin granite slabs were arranged like canvases. The variation in the stones' colour was natural. On the floor, a thicker granite slab was set on the north–south axis. Ultramarine rectangles were painted on the walls.**

◀ *Souterrain*, **by ROSIE LEVENTON** (below right), **was made of scaffolding tubes and boards, and featured a false floor in the shape of a boat hull. It was shown at the Battersea Arts Centre, London, in 1986.**

In 1986 the Museum of Contemporary Art in Ghent, Belgium, invited artists to produce work in 50 houses or rooms offered by volunteers. The exhibition was entitled 'Chambres d'amis' (guest rooms).

➤➤ **HEIKE PALLANCA**'s *Augen – Blicke – Einladung zum Dinner* (Eyes – Views [a pun on Augenblicke, 'blink'] – Invitation to Dinner) (opposite) occupied one of the houses made available for the exhibition. In a darkened room stood a row of cinema seats facing a lightbox containing a photograph which showed a fireplace in an empty room (it was, in fact, the space immediately above, on the next floor). Above the photograph, and also on the right-hand wall, hung smaller lightboxes containing photographs of a pair of eyes observing the spectator.

➤ **MARIA NORDMAN**'s contribution (right), which contained her investigation into the 'questionable hierarchy' of inside and outside, consisted of two rooms on the corner of Hoogport and Belfortstraat (right). A doorway was left deliberately ajar so that passersby could come in. There was no indication on the building that it contained an installation, so visitors entered without preconceptions.

◣ For *Zwei Masken* (Two Masks) (right centre and bottom), **WOLFGANG ROBBE** chose the home of Jean-Paul Deslypere and Charlotte Pannier. He installed three false walls and a ceiling in two internal rooms. The addition partially hid the original interiors, though some elements (picture frame, wall socket) were still visible. Postcards showing both rooms were mounted at the height of the blue dado.

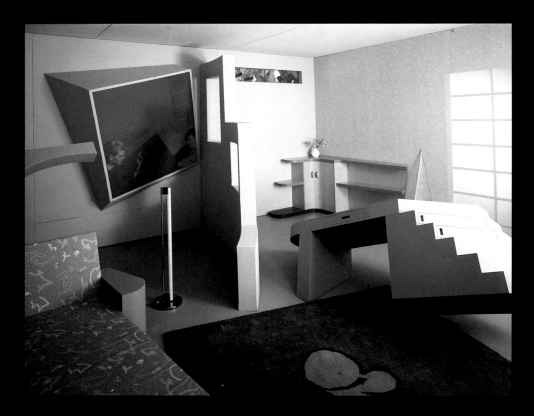

◣ **MARK CAMILLE CHAIMOWITCZ**'s untitled installation above was commissioned by the Arts Council of Great Britain for the Four Rooms exhibition of 1984. To the artist it represents an interior somewhere in the centre of an imaginary city, a mixture of Paris, London and Vienna. He describes it as being 'in one corner of an apartment, on the fourth or fifth floor and on a street junction overlooking both a railway terminus and a market', and continues: 'It is by implication therefore both here yet elsewhere… and although issues of function (both of the artist and from the objects) are queried, the nature of the room is consciously free of role and non specific…hence perhaps, within its purity, a sense of ambiguity or of disquiet.'

In addition to the artists on the preceding pages, the Belgian artist Jan Vercruysse and the Italian artist Luciano Fabro also contributed to the 'Chambres d'amis' exhibition. **JAN VERCRUYSSE** (opposite above) **chose the room of a musician, Johan Grimonprez. In it he placed an empty frame and a black and white photograph of a violin. A third frame was provided by the window.**

The Italian artist **LUCIANO FABRO** used **the living room of Ria and Rik de Keyzer-Bultheel** (opposite below), **who had recently had a baby. Fabro introduced into the room a long white piece of fabric, which the child was allowed to crawl on and play with. He called his interactive installation** C'est la vie.

The works of Serra and Venlet (above and right) **refer to a minimalist tradition. In** Equal and Diagonally Opposite Corners: For Samuel Beckett **(1990), at the Yvon Lambert Gallery, Paris, RICHARD SERRA covered two large canvas panels with a rich brown/black oil paint.**

For his untitled work of 1991 at the Victoria Miro Gallery, London, RICHARD VENLET painted two gallery walls with a layer of high gloss paint, which reflected both the viewers and the room itself.

The ambiguous terrain between artifice and reality is explored in these works, where it can be argued that the concious act of installation in a gallery context makes them art.

Above **RUDOLF STINGEL**'s untitled piece at the Daniel Newburg Gallery, New York, consisted of wall-to-wall fluorescent orange shag-pile carpet, fitted not only in the gallery space, but also in the office, reception area and corridors.

◄ Left **In 1991 the Chicago group HAHA (Richard House, Wendy Jacob, Laurie Palmer and John Ploof) created installations in Daniel Buchholz's apartment in Cologne** (left above) **and in the Daniel Buchholz Gallery** (left). **In the former, Haha installed a fibreboard square which encircled an inner wall and connected the various rooms; in the gallery, they placed a fibreboard desk, occupying the full length of the space, and two standing fans. A smaller, perpendicular desk held the open pages of two Cologne phone books, which the fans blew continuously back**

▲ **GUILLAUME BIJL**'s *Toning Table Centre* was shown at the Isy Brachot Gallery, Brussels, in 1989. Many of Bijl's installations are so convincing that spectators attempt to use the fictional facilities. Here he included fully functional tables, a 'luxurious' red carpet and cheap potted plants. 'Real world' tableaux were depicted in colour photographs on the wall.

Helen Chadwick and Julia Wood occupied non-art spaces in an exploration of the social context of the site.

▲ **HELEN CHADWICK**'s *Blood Hyphen* (above) was the artist's contribution to the London Edge International Biennale in 1988. It was sited in the Woodbridge Chapel, London. Chadwick removed a panel in a pre-existing false ceiling above the pulpit, so that a second space appeared to float above. A blood-red beam of laser light pierced the darkness and lit an enlarged photographic panel showing the artist's blood cells.

➤ In *Cutting Memory*, at the Cartwright Hall, Bradford, in 1988, **JULIA WOOD** (below left and right) **foreshortened the three-dimensional space by the application of red plasticine directly on to the walls, floor and statues. The red rectangular bar visually collapsed the sculptural space into a graphic image.**

➤ *Void Field* by **ANISH KAPOOR** (right) was first made in 1989 and then resited at the British Pavilion, XLIV Venice Biennale, in 1990. The dimensions of the work are variable and the 20 pieces of sandstone were placed according to the volume of the site. Each stone had been hollowed out and coated on the inside with a dense black pigment, creating a void of darkness.

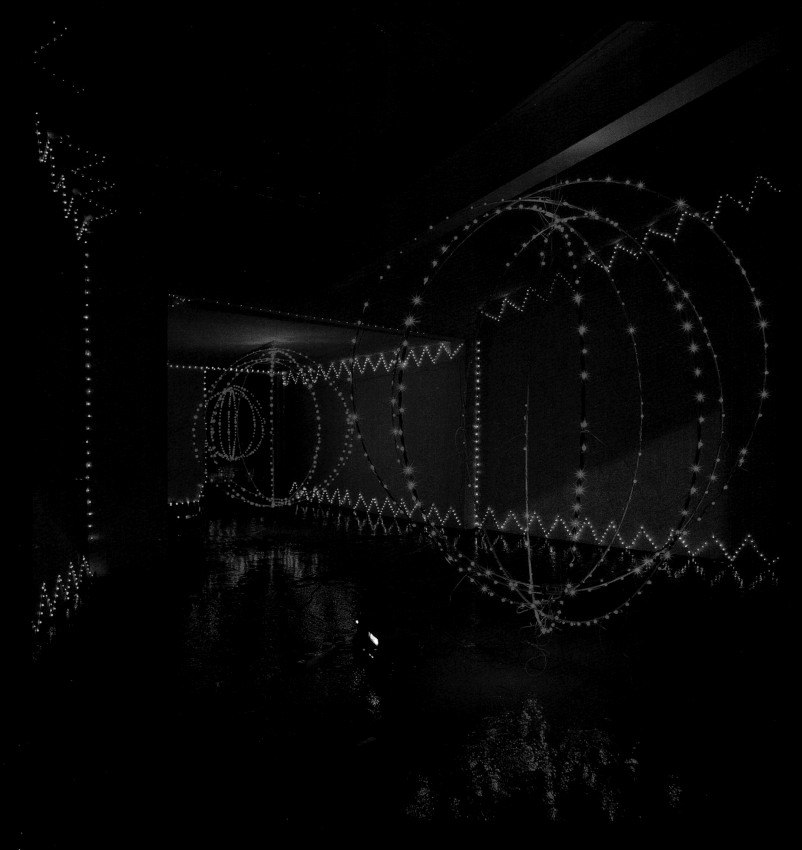

▲ **RON HASELDEN's** *Coliseum* was inspired by the apparently gyrating light sphere that sits on top of the English National Opera building in London, also known as the Coliseum. For the installation at the Showroom Gallery, London, in 1989 (above), light emitting diodes were wired around the spherical shape in the centre, which appeared to rotate as the LED units flickered on and off. The room, framed by similar devices, lost its architectural shape and appeared to expand and contract with each light-pulse.

Comme 2 Roues (Like 2 Wheels) was created by **JEAN-LUC VILMOUTH** in

➤ 1989 for the Naissance d'une Nation (Birth of a Nation) exhibition, Valmy (opposite). The wooden mill and the metal wheel covered with fairground lights stood 35 metres high on a painted wooden floor. Valmy is famous for the day-long battle which led to the proclamation of the Republic.

> In **HIROSHI TESHIGAHARA**'s
Monumental Ikebana (1990) at 65
Thompson Street, New York (opposite
top), **the viewer walked along a curved
path through a tunnel of bamboo.
Teshigahara comes from a line of
Japanese masters of flower arranging,
of which Ikebana is the most avant-
garde form.**

Originally installed in 1969,
◄ **MICHELANGELO PISTOLETTO**'s
Labyrinth (opposite below) **was remade in
different dimensions and layout at the
Paley Wright Gallery, London, in 1991.
On entering, the spectator was
confronted by a maze of corrugated
cardboard at head height.**

**Obsolescent technology is explored in
works by the Chinese artist Gu De Xin
and the German artist Anselm Kiefer.**

▲ **GU DE XIN**'s **untitled work of 1990**
(above) **for the Next Phase exhibition in
London was sited in a disused pumping
station in Wapping. Clear plastic
curtains, in which holes had been
burned, cascaded down from the ceiling
on to rusting industrial equipment.**

> In **ANSELM KIEFER**'s **1991 installation**
Das Grab in den Luften (The Tomb in the
Air) (right) **at the Yvon Lambert Gallery in
Paris, a lead rocket was filled with earth
and lit from inside so that it appeared to
be on fire. Below it were scattered
pieces of lead, glass and earth, while on
the wall a construction of lead, glass and
canvas acted as a backdrop.**

▲ **MARTHA FLEMING** and **LYNE**
▼ **LAPOINTE** site many of their
installations in abandoned buildings.
'The buildings', say the artists, 'are not
cheap and temporary exhibition spaces;
nor are they found objects. They are
ideologically, socially, emotionally, and
economically charged architectures.' For
La Donna Delinquenta (1987) in
Montreal they made use of a theatre
which had been abandoned for 20 years
(above and below). **Fleming and Lapointe
are feminist lesbian lovers as well as
collaborators, and the work explored
representations of women; its title was
taken from a nineteenth-century
criminology text which argued the
innate criminality of the female.**

▲ *The Man Who Flew into Space from His Apartment* (above) **is one tableau from ILYA KABAKOV's installation of 1981-88,** *Ten Characters*. **It has been resited many times and is shown here at the Ronald Feldman Gallery, New York, in 1988. In the intensely claustrophobic room the central object was a slingshot made from old bedsprings and rubbery straps which was positioned beneath a gaping hole in a false ceiling.**

▲ *Two Walls of Fear* (above) by **ILYA KABAKOV** (see also page 61) was installed on a former site of the Berlin Wall. Two parallel wooden structures represented the Eastern and Western walls. Rubbish that had been collected by the artist in the now deserted Potsdamerplatz (the prewar heart of Berlin) hung from wires. Commentary on this debris was printed in German, English and Russian on accompanying white plaques.

➤ *The Missing House* (opposite), by the French artist **CHRISTIAN BOLTANSKI**, was sited in a bombed-out house on the Grosse Hamburger Strasse. On the side walls of two adjacent houses Boltanski installed a series of plaques containing the names and occupations of the former inhabitants of the missing house and their dates of occupation and departure from it. The inhabitants were not killed by the bomb, but were murdered in German death camps.

◄ **RAFFAEL RHEINSBERG** sited *Joint Venture* (left), his contribution to the 1990 'Die Endlichkeit der Freiheit' exhibition, on the Niederkirchnerstrasse in Berlin. He remade a section of the Berlin Wall by lining up 100 wooden telephone cable spools, 50 from the East

nd 50 from the West. They were placed where the wall once separated the Martin Gropius Bau from the former Prussian Parliament.

JANNIS KOUNELLIS, the Greek-born artist, has always been preoccupied with history. For his untitled installation for the same exhibition (left below) he chose a small railway which connected two parts of a factory as a way of commenting on the reunification of Germany. A railcar went back and forth, carrying sacks of coal.

▲ *H.C.W.W.* (1991), by **JANNIS KOUNELLIS,** at the Henry Moore Sculpture Studio in Halifax, England (above), consisted of pillars that bisected the central space. The building had previously been a mill and a hole in the floor exposed the rive

◄ **PAUL HAY's** *Light House* (left), at the University of Western Sydney, was sited near an overground powerline. The excess electricity (electromagnetic radiation) was so great that it activated fluorescent lights mounted on the structure.

◄ **DAVID CRANSTON's** *Reconstructing Nature* (opposite below), on the same campus, consisted of several hundred Australian red gum seedlings in a cross shape. The seedlings were surrounded by weed mats and a red Scotchlite reflector was placed above them. At night a solar powered beacon struck the reflecting tape so that the cross appeared to float in the air, then disappear.

▼ *A Weekend's Worth of Marvellous Illusions* by **JOHN PEPLOW** (below) consisted of two pits one square metre in volume. One was surrounded by quarry tiles and had a gutter grate on top; the other was filled with water and enclosed by a painted steel picket fence.

◄ For the 1990 Tyneside Festival in Gateshead, British artist **PHYLLIDA BARLOW** created *Seam* (opposite above), a huge curve of gold foil installed on a slag heap covered in grass turf.

The works shown here, from an early generation of installation artists with their roots in the 1960s, are to some degree illustrations of concepts.

◄ In *Installation and Paintings* (1990) at the Annely Juda Gallery, London (left), **FRANCOIS MORELLET** uses light as a way of transforming and recording space. Natural light from the skylight affected the intensity of the light-blue neon tubes.

The 5-7-9 Series, an installation of 27 works by **WALTER DE MARIA**, was shown at the Gagosian Gallery, New York, in 1992
◄ (left). Polished stainless steel rods were sunk into black granite bases in sets of three. Each rod was 5, 7 or 9 sided and all possible combinations of these rods were included. The first 'Primary' set contained 6 combinations (5-7-9, 5-9-7, etc.), the second 'Symmetrical' set 9 combinations (5-7-5, 5-9-5, etc.) and the third 'Asymmetrical' set 12 combinations (5-5-7, 5-5-9, etc.). De Maria has often explored mathematical ideas and measurements.

SOL LEWITT's wall works exist as a set of instructions to be enacted by the purchaser, gallery or museum. *Wall Drawing 390* (1983), for the Musée d'Art Contemporain, Bordeaux, was a 16-part drawing of combinations of parallel bands of lines in four directions, executed in India ink. Shown here
◄ (left) are five sets of vertical, horizontal and diagonal lines sited in large archways in the Lainé warehouse, Bordeaux.

➤ **CHRIS JENNINGS**'s *Vault* (1992), at the Museum of Installation, London (opposite), was made intentionally to be entirely reliant on the site. It was composed of metal rods which created a series of arcs which 'defined' the space. It could be seen as a sequence of springs, pushing against the fabric of the building.

▲ Japanese artist **KAZUO KATASE** created *Fisch = Schiff – leer + mehr* (Fish = boat – empty + more) in 1985 at the Kunstforum, Städtische Galerie im Lenbachhaus, Munich (above). A wooden boat filled with liquid was positioned in the centre of the space, with its oars touching the blue-lit walls. A photographic image in negative form stood against the back wall.

◀ In Katase's *Trink eine Tasse Tee* (Have a Cup of Tea) of 1987 (above right), an oversized anodized aluminium teacup was balanced on a rock in the Furka Pass, Switzerland. *Shnee im Frühling* (Snow in Spring) (opposite top), for the

➤ Kunstverein, Kassel, in 1988, consisted of a large blue field impaled by a sword. A butterfly was mounted on the back wall and the entire room was lit by a cool turquoise light.

▼ In **YOKO TERAUCHI**'s *Air Castle* (below), installed in 1991 at the Kanransha Gallery, Tokyo, three black graphite fan-shaped spheres were painted on the walls and floor, representing the intersection of the three dimensions which make up our conventional notion of space. The black conical extension where the three met was covered in bright red pigment and represented a

'fourth dimension'. Terauchi considers this work to be 'unmeasurable', as space is boundless.

◀ The German artist **WOLFGANG LAIB** is shown opposite below installing his contribution to the Falls the Shadow exhibition at the Hayward Gallery, London, in 1986. Laib is known for his use of natural materials. For this work he collected bright yellow pine pollen from the forest, which he dusted in a large rectangle on the floor. In the specially constructed room, visitors were allowed only to view and smell the piece from the entrance.

In these highly ephemeral pieces by three British artists, water is used as a metaphor for the transitory.

◄ ANYA GALLACCIO's installation (left) *In Spite of It All* (1990) placed 21 polished metal tea-kettles on a rustic wooden table in the chimney at the Old Pumping Station, Wapping, London. A constant supply of water produced a cacophony of whistles.

► ROSE FINN-KELCEY's untitled work of 1992 (right) at the Chisenhale Gallery, London, formed part of the Edge exhibition. The sheet-metal base contained heating elements and water, and emitted a hissing sound; above it hung an extractor hood. A cloud of steam hovered between the two, contained in a box of space.

▼ In CRAIG WOOD's untitled installation of 1990 at Building One, London (below), the floor was carpeted with flat plastic envelopes filled with water. The surface appeared to move slightly, and shone with a faint glow.

In *Unity*, by the Scottish artist **CAROLINE WILKINSON** (above), which was installed at the Slaughterhouse Gallery, London, in 1991, three glass sheets etched with enigmatic, fragmentary inscriptions were inserted into the floor. The spectator was required to walk around the piece, since the inscriptions were visible only from the side. One read: 'We see nothing.' Further inscriptions, relating to media comments on the Gulf War, were etched on copper plaques fixed to the wall.

The British artist **GLEN ONWIN** created *As Above, So Below* in 1991 in the derelict Square Chapel, in Halifax. It was a cycle of four works, sited throughout the building, exploring various alchemical processes. In *NIGREDO – Laid to Waste* (opposite), located in the main upper area, the exposed timbers of the roof were reflected in an artificial, concrete pool, filled with a mixture of water, black brine and wax. The lower space, reached by a staircase, held the other three interventions, including *The One to the One – Organic/inorganic* (right), which featured two pools, one containing black brine and white gypsum, the other white brine and black coal. The upper and lower areas were illuminated by a green light.

The disorienting reflective quality of oil was used in these works.

◄ Left **RICHARD WILSON's** *20/50* (1987) was first installed at Matt's Gallery, London, and was resited at the Scottish National Gallery before its purchase in 1987 by the Saatchi Collection. It comprises a shallow steel container with an inserted walkway that enables the viewer to enter the installation. The container is filled with sump oil which acts like a reflecting pool. The density of the oil makes it impossible to estimate its depth.

▲
▼ Above and below Two installations using motor oil, by the Norwegian artist **PER BARCLAY**: *The Jaguar's Cage* (1991), at the Turin Zoo, Italy; and *Old Boathouse* (1990), at Oksefjord, Norway.

GERMANIA

BUNDESREPUBLIK DEUTSCHLAND

PUBBLICA FEDERALE DI GERMANIA

HANS HAACKE's installation *Germania* (above and opposite) **made use of the entire German pavilion at the 1993 Venice Biennale. The visitor was greeted by a photograph of Adolf Hitler which hung at the entrance. The inside of the vast space was empty except for the stone flooring, which had been dug up and then smashed. The work made reference to the memory of a not so distant German past and signalled a warning about the consequences of intolerance and disarray in the new Germany.**

The colonization by artists of the dream and desiring spaces of the media has been of particular political significance. Think, for example, of Barbara Kruger's use of the language of advertising, of Krzysztof Wodiczko's projections or the video installations of Dara Birnbaum, Nam June Paik, Marie-Jo Lafontaine and Gary Hill, and of the words of the U.S. artist Jenny Holzer which you find stuck up in phone booths, flickering across LED displays and pumping out from spectacolor advertising boards:

PROTECT ME FROM WHAT I WANT.

GO WHERE PEOPLE SLEEP AND SEE IF THEY'RE SAFE.

IT TAKES AWHILE BEFORE YOU CAN STEP OVER INERT BODIES AND GO AHEAD WITH WHAT YOU WERE WANTING TO DO.

Although these sentences are not specific, they nevertheless refer in a very direct way to some of the major issues of contemporary existence – AIDS, homelessness, hunger and so on. A key feature of an art like this is that as well as delivering its message, it does so in terms which draw upon the way in which such problems are represented to us in the media. It is the mode of experience that matters, as much as what it is an experience of.

In the 1920s, László Moholy-Nagy recognized that photography provided us with something else besides its extraordinary ability to represent the world. The 'photogram', or 'camera-less record of forms produced by light', freed photographic technology from its dependent, reproductive function and indicated that it was 'in a fair way to bringing (optically) something entirely new into the world'.[1] What Moholy-Nagy's 'paintings with light' reveal is that the manipulation of a medium creates its own space which, unlike the perspectival space of post-Renaissance painting, does not refer to 'real' space but exists alongside it. By extension, many more such 'technological spaces' can be entered by, for example, switching on a video monitor, TV set, turntable, slide projector or tape deck. All these media, in addition to possessing the capability to record and represent an event to a spectator in another time and place to that in which it occurred, engender a mode of experience which is quite particular to themselves.

We inhabit these technological environments as much physically as psychologically, a fact which media theorist Marshall McLuhan perceived clearly. Writing in the early sixties he considered how the possibilities opened up by these new spaces radically undercut the conventional tendency to evaluate cultural experience along the avant garde/kitsch axis. It is the 'depth experience' provided by the electronic media that erodes the importance of distinctions such as 'high' and 'low' because:

A]nything that is approached in depth acquires as much interest as the greatest matters. Because 'depth' means 'in interrelation,' not in isolation. Depth means insight, not point of view; and insight is a kind of mental involvement in process that makes the content of the item seem quite

Some from the loose association of artists around George Maciunas, known as Fluxus and working both in Germany and the U.S., began to explore these media spaces from the late fifties onwards. Nam June Paik in his work, first with sound and subsequently with video, offered situations in which the audience could interact with the technology, constructing their own 'messages' and thereby challenging the impenetrable authority of the media. For Random Access he cut up a spool of recorded tape and stuck the strips haphazardly onto a wall. Playback equipment was provided with a portable head so that one could draw it across the desired sections of tape. Similarly, later set-ups allowed viewers to manipulate magnetic fields or feed sound signals into a TV monitor in order to modify and distort the image on screen. Wolf Vostell incorporated television screens into his paintings.

The limit case of this opening up of new environments, or at least, the one which preoccupies us at present, is the computerized world of virtual reality. Writing of virtual reality or cyberspace technology in 1990, Regina Cornwell said: 'The media has already pounced on it as the psychedelia of the 90s, as the telepornography of the future.'[3] We witness this when, for example, we are privileged with a 'missile's eye view' of the destruction of Baghdad and the computerized target-location of the bomber pilots during the Gulf War. 'This Nintendo war', Aimee Morgana called it.[4] In general, bearing witness to the workings of the mass media by, for example, watching a film or TV programme, or listening to a record, implicates the viewer/listener as a straightforward consumer of spectacle. The majority of the artists in this section, from Peter Fend's proposals for the reshaping of the geopolitical map through Antoni Muntadas's reflection on the phenomenon of television evangelism to Christian Marclay's irreverent treatment of long-playing records, use information technology and the conventions of mass communication to destabilize the authority and power of that spectacle.

What is the role of an audience in installations? In **CHRISTIAN MARCLAY**'s 1989 work at Shedhalle, Zurich (opposite), the discs on the floor had a silent groove. By walking on them, the audience caused scratches and marks, which were then 'playable' as a record of the installation. (The discs were subsequently offered for sale in an edition entitled *Footsteps.)*

▲ **WOLF VOSTELL**'s performances and environments since the 1960s have dealt with the transformation of everyday objects. *Le Cri* (The Cry), created in 1990 (above), was a musical installation for 90 performers, in which 200 disparate objects acted as instruments. Logs were sawn, and the orchestra included a vacuum cleaner section and a television section.

▼ *The Bronx*, by **FABRIZIO PLESSI** (below), was shown in the Aperto section at the 1986 Venice Biennale . Here the audience was completely divorced from the space of the action. Through a metal grating, 26 televisions could be seen, enclosed in metal plates, and with iron shovels embedded in their surfaces. A video showed the reflection of the shovels in pools of water.

▲ The Belgian artist **FRED EERDEKENS** showed his untitled work above at the Museum of Installation, London, in 1991. Light projected through a wire mesh construction cast two separate shadows on the back wall, reading: ADMIRE and REJECT. On the end wall, eleven copper wire twists were inserted and lit by candles. Their shadows spelled out: 'I speak in words and you look at me with sentiment'.

▼ **DAVID DYE**'s *Steps*, of 1988 (below), at the Showroom Gallery, London, used string, lit by ultra-violet fluorescent lights, and mirrors to form what appeared to be solid steps from floor to ceiling. The volumes could only be recognized as being carved out of air when the spectator put a hand into the area of the first step.

▲ *The Transparency of Forms* (1988), by
ANDREA FISHER (above), at the
Showroom Gallery, London, featured
four minimal sculptural elements fixed
to a wall on which was projected a slide
chosen from media images of women
who had been assaulted.

▼ In **DAVID GOLDENBERG**'s *Microwave
and Freezer Stills* of 1992 (below), the
gallery space was reduced to a small
antechamber, wrapped entirely in Cling-
film, separated by two perspex screens
from an identical enclosure opposite.
Two video monitors played indeciph-

erable white noise images. The audience
was monitored by a video camera
installed in the inaccessible mirror-
enclosure. A telephone with numbers of
international galleries was provided,
from which viewers could receive
recorded statements made by the artist.

These installations share a concern with surveying and surveillance, and consequently with control.

▲ The German artist **KLAUS VOM BRUCH**'s preoccupation with technological voyeurism emphasizes its hidden dangers. In *Brattain and Bardeen* (above), shown in 1990-91 at the Daniel Buchholz Gallery, Cologne, two encased video monitors hung from the ceiling and were connected by a pole to the window.

▼ **GARY HILL**'s *Suspension of Disbelief (for Marine)* of 1991-92 (below), for the Doubletake exhibition at the Hayward Gallery, London, consisted of a horizontal bank of 30 black and white video monitors and a video loop. Four computer-controlled tapes shifted images of male and female body parts rapidly across the field of vision.

◀ In **DARA BIRNBAUM**'s *Tiananmen Square: Break-in-Transmission* (1990) (opposite top), at the Museum of Contemporary Art, Ghent, tiny screens suspended from the ceiling showed videos of aspects of the Tiananmen Square massacre: students, journalists, the military. A larger screen scrambled samples from the smaller screens.

➤ *The Chemistry of Love* (1992), by **MICHAEL PETRY** (right) was shown at the James Hockey Gallery, Farnham, England. One hundred and twenty-one Pyrex glass lab vessels, containing the chemical make-up of the human body, hung in an 11-row maze. The head-high monitor played an 11-minute video of a 'scientific sample' of the British population talking about love and lust.

▲ **PETER FEND**'s *Development Plan to Build Albania*, at the Tanja Grunert Gallery, Cologne, in 1992, featured a large three-dimensional earth map of the Albanian tectonic plain. The geographical area spanned several political boundaries (including Montenegro in what was then Yugoslavia) and vividly depicted the chaotic nature of man's desire to impose his own structures on the earth's physical crust. Fend also placed oddly cut up maps of Europe over internationally recognized political boundaries. Television monitors showed live satellite broadcasts of the area. Fend considers his projects to be 'workstations' for the global redistribution of power and resources.

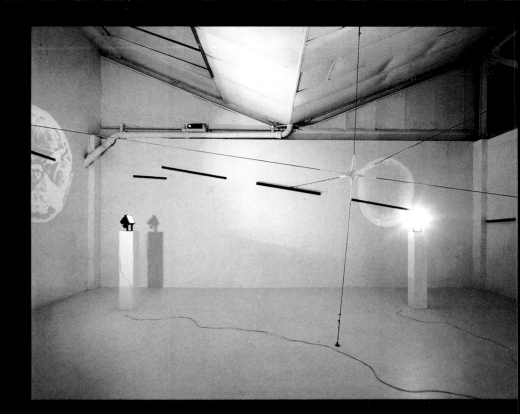

▲ The Polish artist **JAROSLAW KOZLOWSKI**'s *In Yellow* (above) was installed at Matt's Gallery, London, in 1990. The walls, floor and ceiling were painted bright yellow, a colour said to induce breakdown of the will and therefore often used by torturers. On the walls were projections of Kozlowski's brain taken from ultrasound scans. Black lines painted on the walls disorientated the viewer. Metal cables attached to the ceiling, walls and floor were tied together and created a focus at the centre of the room. An electrical cable lay across the floor.

➤ **BILL VIOLA**'s *Theater of Memory* (1985) made use of the space at the Newport Harbor Art Museum, California (right), by projecting a vast image of video static. An uprooted tree, lying on its side, faced the projection. The branches were hung with tiny bells set in motion by electric fans. The gentle chiming of the bells contrasted starkly with the hissing noise made by the screen.

WIR HABEN DIE KUNST DAMIT WIR NICHT AN DER WAHRHE

◀ Belgian artist **MARIE-JO LAFONTAINE** used colour photographic panels of flames for her installation *Wir haben die Kunst damit wir nicht an der Wahrheit zugrunde gehen* (We Have Art so that We Do Not Perish by Truth) at the Stadtsgalerie, Munich, in 1991. The temporary work was sited in the huge dome of the Glyptothek.

▼ *The Complete Works of Jane Austen* (below), **MEG CRANSTON**'s 1991 installation at the Tanja Grunert Gallery, Cologne, consisted of a globe of cream coloured vinyl, 457 cm in diameter, filled with 100,000 litres of air. This volume of air was said to be the amount a person would need while reading Austen's complete works. The globe expanded and contracted depending on the temperature in the gallery.

The U.S. artist **JOSEPH KOSUTH** has explored the structure of language and the language of signs in various conceptual formats.

▲ **'(A Grammatical Remark)', 1988**, a series of works by Kosuth, was made directly onto the gallery wall. It has been remade several times. The latest version (above), **shown in 1991 at the Rubin** Spangle Gallery, New York, featured typewriter-face text and blue neon on black walls.

◄ **Zero & Not**, also a series, has been shown in many venues, with the cancelled text in the appropriate language. The German version is seen opposite above **at the Sigmund Freud Museum, Vienna.**

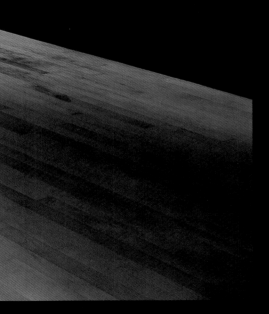

A grammatical remark))

➤ In 1991 Kosuth was commissioned by the French Ministry of Culture to create a work commemorating Jean-François Champollion, the chief decoder of Egyptian hieroglyphics. In *Ex Libris – J.F. Champollion (Figeac)* (right), Kosuth reproduced the Rosetta stone in black granite. The 100 square metres of granite function as a series of steps which visitors ascend.

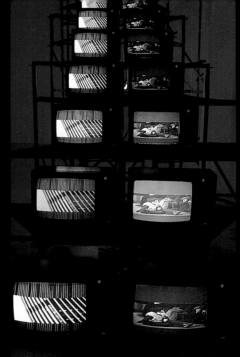

Many installation artists have appropriated technology as a fundamental part of their work.

▲ The Korean-born **NAM JUNE PAIK** created *V-MATRIX with Beuys' voice am Seibu 1983-88* at the Hayward Gallery, London (above). The V-shaped wooden frame held 55 video monitors programmed to display images from a Joseph Beuys performance, in which Paik had collaborated.

◄ **TINA KEANE**'s *Escalator* (1988) at the Riverside Studios, London (above right), took the form of two escalators with two sides (or screens). One side depicted images of wealthy life, the other – on the down escalator – showed homeless people sleeping in London Underground (subway) stations.

▼ In **SUSAN TRANGMAR**'s *Lines of Flight* (1988) (below), at the Chisenhale Gallery, London, images were projected on to

gallery surfaces, some into corners, others at oblique angles.

➤ *The Endless Conveyor* by **MAX COUPER** (right) was shown at the Museum of Installation, London, in 1990. The audience was carried on the conveyor belt past a wall of back-projected images, animated by a computerized programme. The sequence comprised 486 slides on six projectors and was accompanied by a soundtrack of almost inaudible whispers.

Two Catalan artists, both based in New York, have consistently addressed structures and icons of power.

◀ In *Dromos Indiana* (1989), his reinterpretation of the Indiana War Memorial's Tomb of the Unknown Soldier, at the Indiana State Museum, **FRANCESC TORRES** hung a large-scale American flag above the centrally located video installation (opposite).

▼ A 1963 Ferrari Indianapolis in mint condition (below) and a plaster reproduction of a Greco-Roman horse's head (reminiscent of the Ferrari mascot) were positioned on top of a horizontal bank of 40 video monitors showing a 3-channel synchronized video which linked the themes of machismo, patriotism and war. Two glass cases, one containing a racing helmet, the other a green army issue helmet, were placed at either end of the cars.

▲ **ANTONI MUNTADAS**'s *The Board Room* (1987) at Kent Fine Art, New York (above), consisted of 13 chairs – an echo of the Last Supper – placed around a boardroom table. Behind each chair hung a photograph of a religious leader, in whose mouth was a small video monitor showing the leader speaking. The subjects included the Ayatollah Khomeini, Billy Graham, Sun Myung Moon and Pope John Paul II.

Like other forms of art, installation is sometimes a kind of political activism.

◄ The Polish-born artist **KRZYSZTOF WODICZKO** projects images on to public buildings in an attempt to address their status as power symbols. In 1990 he projected a man holding a gun in one hand and a candle in the other on the front of the Hirshhorn Museum in Washington, D.C. (left).

► **CHRIS BURDEN's** *All the Submarines of the United States of America* (1987), shown at the Newport Harbor Art Museum, California, featured 625 miniature cardboard submarines suspended from the ceiling (opposite). The quantity matched the number of submarines in the U.S. fleet at the time. The names of the submarines were painted on an adjacent wall.

◄ *Missiles and Bunnies* by **PAUL THEK** was installed at the Hirshhorn Museum, Washington, D.C., in 1984. Composed of three tableaux (the main one shown left), it was a playful, ironic piece, preoccupied with turning scavenged trivia into spectacle.

► In 1978 **MIERLE LADERMAN UKELES** became the first artist-in-residence at New York's Sanitation Department. *Touch Sanitation*, which she created in 1984, was shown both at the Ronald Feldman Gallery, New York, and at a condemned New York Sanitation Department collection pier. It featured several tableaux. At the Ronald Feldman Gallery, stacks of videos, the U.S. and state flags, and imagery painted on the walls and ceilings (clocks, trash pick-up points) combined to explore the subject of waste disposal (opposite). The videos showed Ukeles' encounters with sanitation workers and documented her attempt to shake the hand of everyone employed by the department.

These three U.S. artists see language as a seat of knowledge and power.

▲ In her untitled 1991 installation at the Mary Boone Gallery, New York (above), **BARBARA KRUGER** covered the gallery's walls, floor and ceiling with imagery and text relating to violence against women and minorities. Viewers had to walk on the covered floor to see the work in its entirety, thus placing themselves directly within it.

▼ In *Bric-a-Brac* (below), at the Stux Gallery, New York, in 1990, **CARY LEIBOWITZ** (the gay artist known as 'Candyass') satirized the use of slogans on merchandise, replacing clichés with subversive messages such as 'Life Sucks' and 'Loser Line Forms Here'. Issues of sexuality and gender were referred to in a wall plaque, which read: 'But he wanted people to like him or at least not look at him in a way like they knew he was thinking about sucking cock all day.'

▼ **JENNY HOLZER**'s *Under a Rock* (1986/89) (below) is seen here at the Institute of Contemporary Arts, London. It consisted of LED (light emitting diode) screens, from which messages were flashed at the viewer, and black granite spotlit benches, on which the same messages were engraved. The theme was apocalyptic, with texts such as: YOU SPIT ON THEM BECAUSE THE TASTE LEFT ON YOUR TEETH EXCITES. YOU SHOWED HOPE ALL OVER YOUR FACE FOR YEARS AND THEN KILLED THEM IN THE INTERESTS OF TIME.

Some artists have seen installation as a way of uniting art and theatre, culminating in works presented as 'spectacles'.

▼ The Spanish artist **ANTONI MIRALDA** created the *Honeymoon Project* to celebrate the 'marriage' of the Statue of Liberty, New York, to the Column of Christopher Columbus in Barcelona, in 1992, the 400th anniversary of the 'discovery' of the Americas. The project spanned six years, beginning in 1986, when the mayor of New York gave his blessing to the couple's engagement, and ending in 1992 with the wedding ceremony in Las Vegas. Two works from the project are shown here: *The Wedding*
◄ *Cake* (left), exhibited in Paris in 1989, and *The Eternity Ring* (below), shown in 1991 in Birmingham, England; the latter was floated from the city's jewelry quarter through the city centre, to be eventually installed at the Ikon Gallery. It was later taken to New York for the nuptial procession.

➤ **STATION HOUSE OPERA** combine theatre and sculpture. In *The Bastille Dances*, of 1989, in Cherbourg, France (opposite), for the Bicentennial celebrations, their performance included building a structure from thousands of concrete breeze-blocks to rival the town hall in the background (unseen). The structure was built and disassembled in a matter of hours.

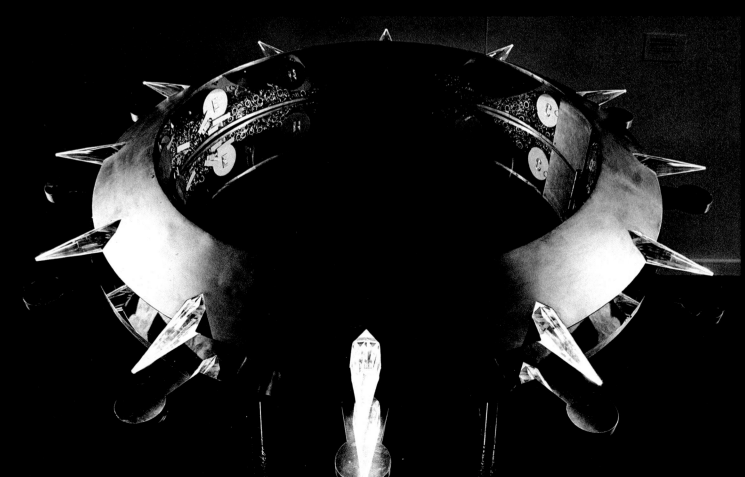

The line between performance art and installation is often blurred and in
➤ **MATTHEW BARNEY**'s installations every piece implies performance. Barney's works combine action with video, sculpture and sports-related artefacts. In *Field Dressing* or *Transexualis* at the Stuart Regen Gallery, Los Angeles, in 1991 (right), the apparently solid objects were made from frozen petroleum jelly (vaseline). A video which was played during the exhibition showed a naked Barney hanging by mountaineering clips and ropes from the gallery ceiling. The artist masturbated and autosodomized on the objects he had created.

▶ The Danish group **HOTEL PRO FORMA** –
▶ composed of artists, musicians, architects and scientists – produce works that are a cross between an installation and a performance. *Fact-Arte-Fact* (left and above left), performed in 1991 at the Royal Museum of Fine Art, Copenhagen, contained five pairs of identical twins and six installation environments. It addressed notions of human singularity, loss of identity, genetic engineering, and aspects of perspective and illusion.

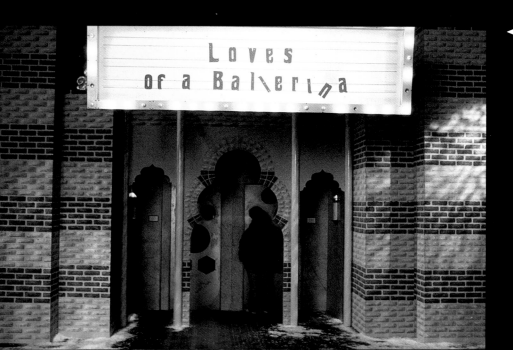

◀ **ELEANOR ANTIN** has created a role for herself as an imaginary black ballerina, Elenora Antinora, a member of Sergei Diaghilev's Ballets Russes. Antinora was the subject of Antin's filmic installation *Loves of a Ballerina* at the Ronald Feldman Gallery, New York, in 1986 (left)

➤ **SHIN EGASHIRA's** *Male and Female on the Bed Looking at the Window* (right) was created for the 1991 Venice Biennale of Architecture, and remade at the Camden Arts Centre, London. It highlighted the artist's concern with the subject of intimacy and the relationship of outside to inside. The installation's complex and precise workings were based on the particular narrative denoted by the title, in which two lovers looked through a window at a cat in a flowerbed, and the cat in turn looked at a fish in a pond. The scene, translated into a machine with moving parts, was relayed by video link to a separate room.

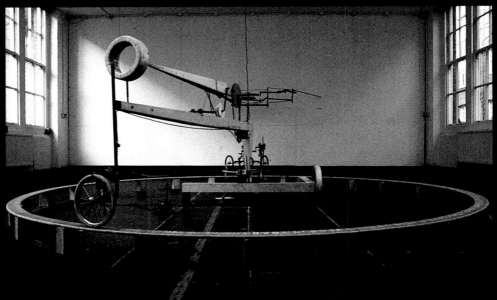

◀ *Massao (missoes)* (How to Build Cathedrals) was installed at the Institute of Contemporary Arts, London, in 1987 (left). It is a comment by the Brazilian artist **CILDO MEIRELLES** on the structure of the Catholic Church. Two thousand bones were hung above 600,000 metal coins linked by a chain of 800 communion wafers. The coins were ringed by 86 paving stones and the whole work was shrouded in a black veil.

▶ **ANN HAMILTON**'s *Offerings* (below left), for the 1991 Carnegie International, occupied a derelict house in the once thriving mining community of Pittsburgh. The house acted as a cage for a flock of canaries (the traditional miners' bird). The vitrine, placed in the top room, contained votive wax heads which were melted under heat lamps so that the wax dripped through to the floor below.

◀ **AIMEE MORGANA**'s *Room for Hope* (opposite above) was shown at the Pat Hearn Gallery, New York, in 1991. On a rug of grass stood a bed surrounded by four black-draped posts. Black iron poles prevented entry. The gilt, mirrored 'Reality Test' headboard held lighted candles and *gris-gris* voodoo talismans; the 'Wishful Thinking' pillows were covered in roses; the 'Security Blanket' quilt was a patchwork of black velvet and gold condom packets.

▶ **LOUISE BOURGEOIS'** tableaux delve deeply into the subconscious. She has created a series of works called *Cells*, one of which, *Cell (Arch of Hysteria)* (1989–93) was shown at the 1993 Venice Biennale (opposite below). The artist has said of this work: 'Each Cell deals with fear… The Cell with the figure or arch of hysteria deals with emotional and psychological pain. Here … pleasure and pain are merged in a state of happiness. Her arch – the mounting of tension and the release of tension – is sexual. It is a substitute for orgasms with no access to sex.'

These installations explore the fragility of bodily experience.

◄ **GENEVIEVE CADIEUX's** *La Felûre, au choeur des corps* (Fracture in the Chorus of the Bodies) was installed in the Canadian Pavilion at the 1990 Venice Biennale (left). Twenty-two photographic panels showing close-ups of parts of the body in evocative poses were inserted in the windows of the pavilion.

Lizart, **TUNGA's** installation for the
► Whitechapel Art Gallery, London, in 1989 (opposite), resembled a gigantic circuit. The 'current' appeared to be carried by braided, reptilian wires through storage plates shaped like enormous combs.

LUCIA NOGUEIRA's untitled installation at the Unit 7 Gallery, London, in 1988
▼ (below) appeared at first to consist of two empty spaces. On closer inspection pieces of black fur could be seen appearing from the floorboards, from under a false wall, and from the ends of open pipes and electrical sockets. Rubber tubes emerged from some of the knotholes in the floor; other holes were bandaged and plugged. Shown here is a detail of the floorboards.

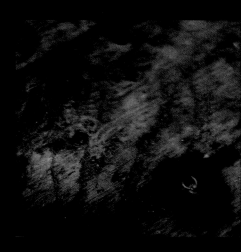

◄ **DAMIEN HIRST's** preoccupation with life and death was demonstrated in *In & Out of Love* (left), shown at the Tamara Chodzko Gallery, London, in 1991. Hirst fitted the upstairs gallery with large white canvases, plants and the cocoons of exotic butterflies. Radiators raised the temperature to that required for the butterflies to hatch. They died shortly after, completing their life cycle. The paintings had dead butterflies embedded into their surfaces.

▲ *In the Shadow of the City...Vamp RY* by
JUDITH BARRY (above) was shown at
the Institute of Contemporary Arts,
London, in 1991. Focusing on the urban
experience, this slide film installation
presented simultaneous views of public
places and domestic scenes. The still
slide projections were inset with four
small Super-8 images.

▼ **ROGER WELCH's** *Drive In: Second
Feature* (1982), first exhibited in New
York at the Whitney Museum of Art,
(left) consisted of a full-scale 1958
Cadillac ElDorado Biarritz, made of tree
branches, bamboo and twine. A 12-
minute film was shown periodically,
consisting of trailers for and
advertisements from films of the 1950s.

➤ **RAIMUND KUMMER's** *Wild Card* was
originally made for a one-night show at
the Goethe House in New York
(opposite). A full-length, double-exposed
photo of the artist was fastened to the
lid of a Steinway piano. The room re-
sounded to the tapping of a blind man's
cane, previously recorded in the same
space by the artist, working in the dark.

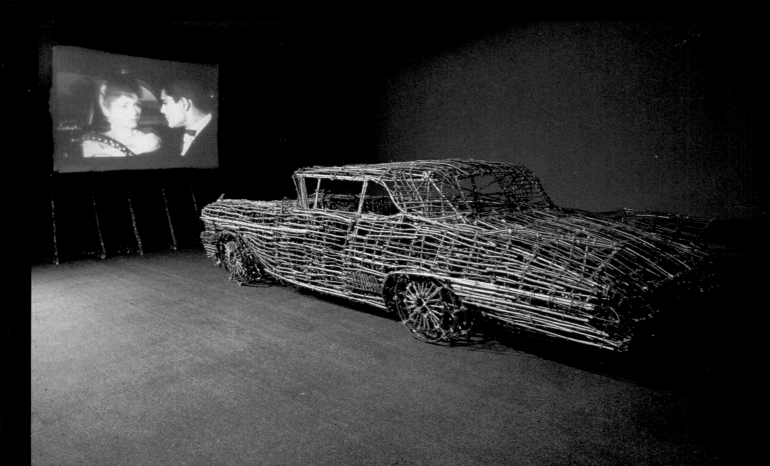

▲ **JONATHAN BOROFSKY**'s dream-based installations use a variety of materials and styles. At the Yvon Lambert Gallery, Paris, in 1991 (above), he installed four metal and red glass *Heart Light* sculptures, from the bases of which came the sound of a heartbeat. On the walls hung paintings of the light spectrum, entitled *Light of Consciousness*. Scattered on the floor were flyers printed by Borofsky, referring to a strike taking place in Paris at the time.

▼ *Charon (the M.I.T. Project),* by the Irish artist **JAMES COLEMAN**, was shown at the Lisson Gallery, London, in 1989. It was a 20-minute high-definition colour slide presentation with accompanying recorded sound narration, which depicted the fictional lives of several photographers. These included (below) a man who was obsessed with restaging car wrecks.

▲ The Heimat exhibition was organized by the Wewerka & Weiss Gallery, Berlin, in 1990-91. It took place in the then divided cities of East and West Berlin and featured the work of twelve artists from eight countries. It consisted mostly of site-specific installations dealing with the theme of homeland, or origin.

The Way It Was (1990-91), by ALFREDO JAAR, at the Galerie Vier, East Berlin (above), was created for the exhibition.

Jaar took three photographs from one of the gallery's windows of the opposite building, cars and passersby. The cibachromes were then placed in custom-made lightboxes that fitted the gallery's three windows.

◀ Left **REBECCA HORN**'s *The Hydra-Forest/performing: Oscar Wilde* was shown at the Carnegie Museum of Art, Pittsburgh, as part of the 1988 Carnegie International. The installation contained glass, mercury and an electrical chandelier that sparked continuously. The two sides of the antler-like ceiling wires were connected by a live current.

➤ Opposite **SARKIS**' *Elle danse dans l'atelier de Sarkis avec le quatuor No 15 de Dimitri Shostakovich* (She danced around Sarkis' studio to the Dimitri Shostakovich quartet No 15) was part of the Heimat exhibition at the Wewerka & Weiss Gallery, Berlin, in 1990 (see also page 113). A clay sculpture sat on a kilim placed over a video monitor. Playing continuously was a tape of the Borodin Quartet performing the piece mentioned in the title. Also included were Sarkis' personal mementoes and earlier pieces by the artist.

◀ Opposite below **The Belgian artist MARIANNE BERENHAUT** has created a series of installations entitled *Vie privée*. This work was shown at La Gare du Watermael, Brussels, in 1989. Artefacts of an interior life are juxtaposed with 'the passing car', represented by the automobile wing.

▲ Above **In ANGELA BULLOCH**'s untitled work at the Castella di Rivoli, Turin, in 1989, spherical lights were placed at the points where the arches met the walls. The spheres lit up at varying intervals, setting up an atmosphere of internal conversation.

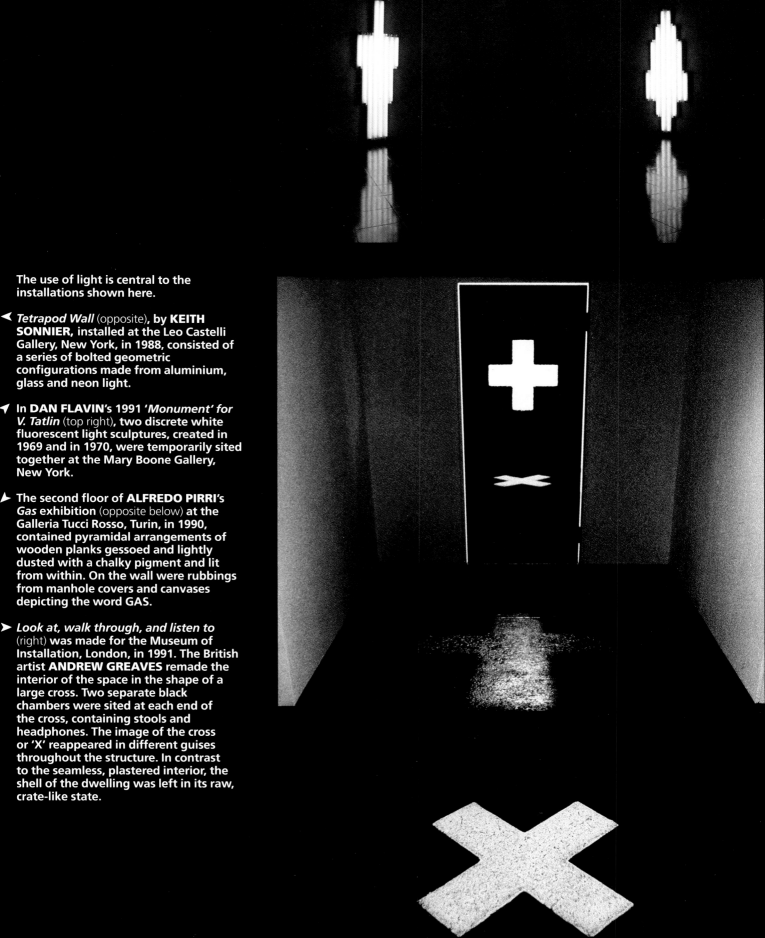

The use of light is central to the
installations shown here.

◄ *Tetrapod Wall* (opposite), **by KEITH
SONNIER, installed at the Leo Castelli
Gallery, New York, in 1988, consisted of
a series of bolted geometric
configurations made from aluminium,
glass and neon light.**

◄ **In DAN FLAVIN's 1991** *'Monument' for
V. Tatlin* **(top right), two discrete white
fluorescent light sculptures, created in
1969 and in 1970, were temporarily sited
together at the Mary Boone Gallery,
New York.**

➤ **The second floor of ALFREDO PIRRI's**
Gas **exhibition** (opposite below) **at the
Galleria Tucci Rosso, Turin, in 1990,
contained pyramidal arrangements of
wooden planks gessoed and lightly
dusted with a chalky pigment and lit
from within. On the wall were rubbings
from manhole covers and canvases
depicting the word GAS.**

➤ *Look at, walk through, and listen to*
(right) **was made for the Museum of
Installation, London, in 1991. The British
artist ANDREW GREAVES remade the
interior of the space in the shape of a
large cross. Two separate black
chambers were sited at each end of
the cross, containing stools and
headphones. The image of the cross
or 'X' reappeared in different guises
throughout the structure. In contrast
to the seamless, plastered interior, the
shell of the dwelling was left in its raw,
crate-like state.**

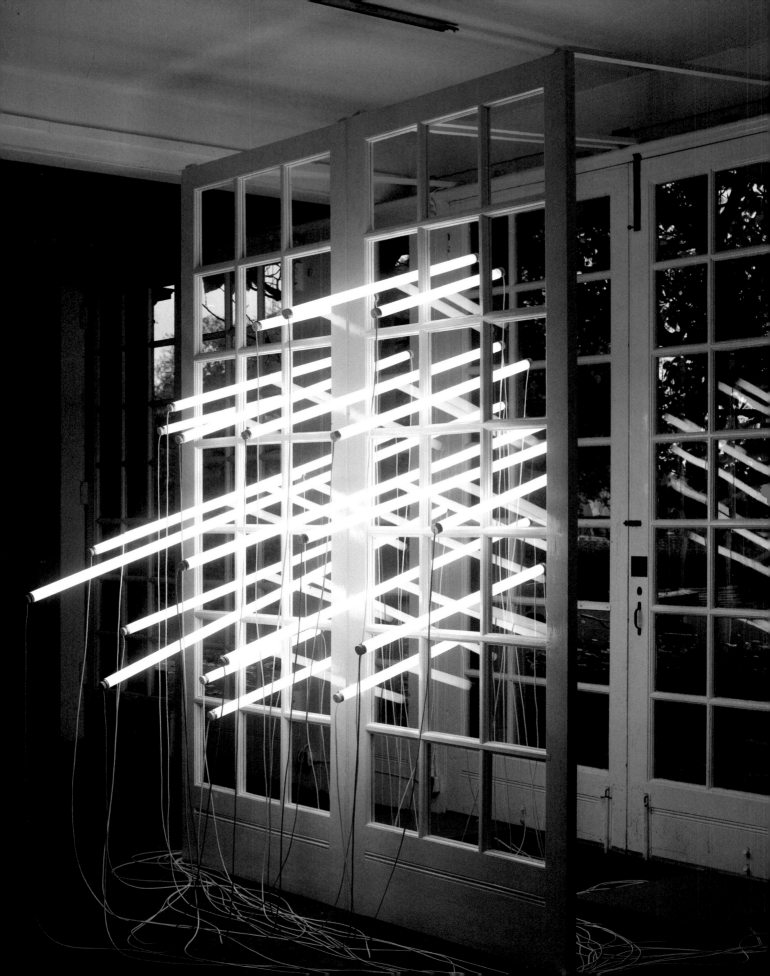

◄ **BILL CULBERT**'s *An Explanation of Light: The Serpentine Windows* (opposite) **was installed at the Serpentine Gallery, London, in 1983. Fluorescent tubes were mounted at an angle and projected through a false window. The latter was hung in front of the full-length french windows that open on to the park in which the gallery is located. Culbert's false window, with its electric light, was reflected in the real window and the tubes appeared to project out into the park as far as the actual tubes projected into the gallery. For his**
▲ **installation at Gateshead** (above) **for the 1990 Tyneside International Exhibition, Cuthbert took over a new, but as yet uninhabited, house. The fluorescent tubes were used on this occasion to bathe the upstairs space in cool light.**

➤ Fluorescent light was also used by **BRUCE NAUMAN** in his *Changing Light Corridor with Rooms* (right), originally created in 1972 and installed in the Anthony d'Offay Gallery in 1988. A long, very narrow corridor was framed by fluorescent light. Branching off it was a rectangular room and a triangular room, whose only access was visual, via the corridor.

▶ ▶ **CORNELIA PARKER's** *Cold Dark Matter –*
An Exploded View, of 1991, featured an
ordinary English garden shed and its
contents, which the artist exhibited at
the Chisenhale Gallery, London (top left),
before having them removed to an army
site where they were blown up. The
resulting fragments were then
▶ rearranged in the gallery, hanging from

thin wires (centre left). The essence of the shed was retained, as was the explosive nature of its destruction.

◄ **JOHN COLEMAN**'s *Lapwing Redwing Fieldfare* (below left), shown in 1992 at the Museum of Installation, London,

artist called 'arcane travellers' projected on the museum walls. These were created by mounting small mirrors on the floor with the figures blacked out on the surface. A strong light projected the silhouette on to the walls. In the process of viewing the installation, the visitors' shadows interacted with the figures on

▲ In **CHRISTIAN BOLTANSKI**'s *Les Ombres* (The Shadows), at the Musée de Nice in 1986 (above), tiny figures hung in the centre of the space, suspended from a wire structure and lit gently at floor level. The images were projected on to the surrounding walls, where they appeared as surreal and macabre

The harnessing of different forms of energy to create a sense of metamorphosis and uncertainty is demonstrated in these works.

◄ In **PIERPAOLO CALZOLARI**'s untitled work of 1990 at the Gentili Gallery, Florence (opposite), a large sheet of copper, suspended from the ceiling, was attached to a similar-sized folded lead base and linked to a cooling apparatus.

The cooling apparatus froze the adjoining pipe and turned the left-hand side of the copper sheet white.

▲ **MAURIZIO MOCHETTI**'s *Quartz Spheres* of 1989 (above) at the Edward Totah Gallery, London, consisted of 44 quartz spheres, through which a red laser passed, illuminating them as if from within. In viewing the work, the spectator disrupted the beam.

▼ In **MONA HATOUM**'s 1989 installation *Light at the End* (below), at the Showroom Gallery, London, an iron metal frame held six vertical heating elements. As the viewer moved into the narrowing space, an intense heat was given off by what appeared to be a light source. Only on reaching the grille did the viewer become aware that the light and heat sources were one.

There are two linked elements to this section. Firstly there is the way in which installation, as the arrangement of things within a gallery environment, overlaps and/or interferes with the activity of exhibition organizing. In this regard there are two works by Duchamp that should be mentioned. The first, made for the 1938 International Exhibition of Surrealism in Paris was *1,200 Bags of Coal*; the second was the *Mile of String* installed around the 'First Papers of Surrealism' show at 551 Madison Avenue in 1942. What was significant about both these works was that they were not discrete, set among the other contributions, but instead took the entire exhibiting space and its contents as their arena. The bags of coal were fixed to the ceiling while in the middle of the floor below them a single brazier was placed, glowing with the light from a bulb. (Safety considerations precluded actually lighting a fire in the brazier.) What Duchamp achieved in effect was to turn the entire space on its head by putting the floor on the ceiling and the light source on the floor. Similarly, the tangle of twine running to and from all points of the room in the later exhibition demanded not only that spectators actively *participate* in viewing the exhibition, but also determined that their view of the show would be conditioned before all else by Duchamp's intervention.

Starting in 1951 with 'Growth and Form', Richard Hamilton organized, alone and in collaboration with other members of the Independent Group, a number of exhibitions over the following decade. The last in this sequence was 'an Exhibit' in 1957. Rather than presenting material related to a particular theme, the subject of this exhibition was itself. It consisted of flat, rectangular panels of various sizes and colours, transparent, translucent and opaque, suspended from the ceiling on an orthogonal grid:

The installation was empirical; no plans were preconceived and the position of each panel was determined solely as a result of consideration of the space and location of earlier placement of panels. Each installation would result in a completely different improvisation to create a constructivist work of art on an environmental scale.[1]

A spectator walking through the exhibition space was therefore greeted by a constantly changing set of abstract relationships between different elements.

The self-consciousness promoted by projects of this kind, the awareness of the kind of experience that visiting an exhibition entails, leads on to the second, larger factor: a questioning of the status of the museum. What we think about objects is intimately connected to their physical disposition for viewing – their grouping, ordering, juxtaposition and so on. Systems of classification, far from being objective structures, carry within themselves the prejudices and assumptions of those who devise and use them. Lothar Baumgarten is one who has used naming to reveal the sites of power and oppression, but also of aspiration, in contemporary culture.[2] Some of the artists in this section – Thomas Locher's thesaurus-like sets of linguistic permutations, Mike Kelley's soft toy arrangements, Wim Delvoye's imaginary countries, Adrian Piper's, David Hammons's and Rasheed Araeen's deconstructions of racial stereotyping – use systems against themselves as a way of challenging received wisdom about the way things are. Beyond this, though, an unresolvable but fruitful antagonism exists within any museum between its invitation to view an object in the context provided by all the other exhibits, and the requirement that each object be taken separately. (The museum, after all, is a monument to the removal of objects from their cultural context.) Museum-based installation works with this tension, proposing an erasure of the distinction between what has traditionally been the museum's object of attention – the remnant or relic – and that which is newly offered for scrutiny (Haim Steinbach's shelf arrangements, or Ian Hamilton Finlay's campaigns to reinvigorate presocratic virtue).[3]

The imaginary museum run by Marcel Broodthaers between 1968 and 1972 is instructive here. It was initiated, according to Broodthaers, in response to the social and political unrest of 1968. Over the next few years, the display of its various mythical sections provided a critique of the structures of institutional power through which the museum is able to promote its version of history. Throughout the period of its existence, Broodthaers' museum mockingly took the eagle as its symbol. Broodthaers' operated on the ground prepared by Marcel Duchamp with his readymades. He though, inspired by his fellow-Belgian, René Magritte, moved in the opposite direction to Duchamp in an effort to dissolve art's grip on objects. The text from Magritte's famous *Trahison des Images*, a picture of a pipe under which is written 'Ceci n'est pas une pipe', was taken up and altered by Broodthaers into a contra-Duchampian slogan: in the final version of his *Museum of Modern Art*, shown in Düsseldorf in 1972, Broodthaers displayed a huge range of objects, all of them bearing the image of an eagle and each accompanied by a label stating, 'This is not a work of art'. This was the case even for those items borrowed from places such as the Louvre and the British Museum, and which therefore had aesthetic provenance. The museum was a fiction, displaying nothing but the symbol of that authority whereby museums everywhere present their version of things.

To talk about my museum means discussing the ways and means of analyzing fraud. The ordinary museum and its representatives simply present one form of the truth. To talk about this museum means speaking about the conditions of truth. It is also important to find out whether or not the fictional museum casts a new light on the mechanisms of art, the artistic life, and society. I pose the question with my museum.[4]

Michael Asher's work has also been central to the elaboration of our attitude towards the museum as a site within which to make and view art. In a series of installations made in the seventies, culminating in two works made in Chicago in 1979, Asher, through revealing the historical dimension to the process of looking, brought the interior and exterior of the gallery into contact. Even an action as simple as peeling the white paint from a gallery's walls – done to the Toselli Gallery, Milan, in 1973 – had significant implications. Asher explains:

Curiously enough, the white painted surface always covered over a much richer surface underneath. The complete removal, a subtractive condition, became additive with the exposure of the plaster. With the notion of exposure, other variables concerning the gallery and its surroundings became recognized. Plaster, left as unpainted surface, is mostly found outdoors. By sand-blasting the wall surfaces, I essentially brought the recollection of an outdoor material indoors.[5]

AMERICA *Invention* (1988-1993), a site-specific work by **LOTHAR BAUMGARTEN,** was installed in 1993 at the Solomon R. Guggenheim Museum, New York.

This particular wall work was created for Frank Lloyd Wright's rotunda, where it was painted into the architectural context of the double helix itself. Its artistic grammar was developed from the organic structure of the rotunda's module. The painted space contained a discourse about the 'misnaming' of the 'New World' by Europeans. The structure of the spiral had been divided into meridians and longitude lines. Through this division the space became a globe, a cosmic space, and, by 'naming' North and South American native peoples, a map of the Americas.

The rhythm of the alternating right side up and upside down 'names', written in blue, red and black, was interrupted by five yellow segments which were horizontally painted on the bulge of the spiral. This horizon made the incline visible and the viewer aware of his/her own physical condition. They provided a concept of landscape and through their cylindrical shape the figure of 'maize' was suggested, a metaphor for life and the 'New World'. Like ripples generated from stones thrown into the water, they mingled with each other and echoed the anthropological, common names of the native societies of the Americas. At the High Gallery twelve mandorla shaped sections of longitudinal lines represented the colonial conflict between different cultures. Formed from adverbs, they signify the clash between two different systems of thinking and were collected from late-1980s anthropological publications. These words were painted alternately in green, black and grey, the colours of U.S. paper money.

PAIUTE

NAVAJO

ARAPAHO

APACHE

MIWOK

PIM

borrowed land for sale

The function of the museum and its ability to bestow status on an art work is a topic of particula[r] interest and in these works is addressed in the museum's own language.

▲ For *The Abandonment of Origins* (1990) at the Mappin Art Gallery, Sheffield, **SHARON KIVLAND** and **BEN HILLWOOD-HARRIS** (above) placed reconstructions of found artefacts on a series of white plinths. Drawings of the objects and the 'strata' in which they were found were also displayed. The works dealt with the fictitious nature of cultural history and the way in which the placing of objects in a museum setting empowers them with meaning and value.

◄ *The Reign of Narcissism* by **BARBARA BLOOM** (left) was first exhibited at the Museum of Contemporary Art, Los Angeles, and is shown here at the Serpentine Gallery, London, in 1990. Most of the objects in the fictional museum room bore the image of the artist: plaques, busts, cameos, etc. The museum shop sold Bloom's limited edition chocolates, champagne and postage stamps.

▼ **MICHAEL ASHER**'s intervention in the Hall of Architecture at the Carnegie Museum, Pittsburgh, created for the 1991 Carnegie International (below) sat on four circular radiators. The apparently random letters were in fact acronyms of companie[s] that test materials used in the production of art objects. The letters were made from plaster of paris, the material that had been traditionally used in the production of the casts found in the Hall.

◄ **ADRIAN PIPER**'s work since the 1960s has explored overt and latent racism, often through confrontations with members of the public. In *Cornered*, of 1988 (left), a 17-minute video of Piper was placed in the corner of the John Weber Gallery, New York, with an upended table braced against it. On the wall hung two framed birth certificates, both registering the birth of Piper's father, one describing him as black and the other as white. Three chairs were provided for viewing the work. Piper addressed the audience, beginning with the statement 'I'm black,' and adding '… if you feel that my letting you know that I'm not white is making an unnecessary fuss… you must feel that the right and proper course of action for me to take is to pass for white…'.

▲ In 1988, the Yugoslavian artist **BRACO**
◄ **DIMITRIJEVIC** took a photograph of a passerby on London's Waterloo Bridge and made it into a banner which was hung outside the nearby Hayward Gallery (above and left). The super-human scale of *The Casual Passer-By I Met* served to question the status of public images.

▲ **TIM HEAD**'s *The Tyranny of Reason* (1985) at the Institute of Contemporary Arts, London, filled the gallery's ground floor with imagery relating to surveillance and oppression. Slide projectors placed on standard grey metal shelving units threw corporate identity logos on to the walls. Security mirrors were positioned throughout the structure and barbed wire was fastened to the top of the shelves. A loud soundtrack increased the level of tension in the area, as did the rapid rate at which the slides flickered on and off.

◄ **DAVID IRELAND**'s *Repository* (left) was created for his 1988 retrospective exhibition at the Art Museum of the University of California at Berkeley. In his work, Ireland recontextualizes mundane material. *Repository* featured an ordinary filing cabinet containing folders wrapped in chicken wire.

▲ **LOUISE SUDELL**'s 1992 installation
▼ *Second Skin* (above, left and right)
developed her interest in the scientific
exploration of the body. Layers of
white sheeting, snakeskins, facial peels,
and wigs made from the artist's hair
surrounded the viewer on three floors.

Writing on the nature of human skin,
Sudell has stated that 'Its beauty is
imbedded in its transience, its own
vulnerability to mortality'. *Second Skin*
was housed in a disused building,
previously the Archive for Foreign
Affairs, in the Hague.

Both Hansjorg Schafer and Robert Gober
have raised the issue of reality versus
deception, the first by using actual
household objects as building blocks for
his structures, the second by making
things look as if they are readymade
when in fact they are constructed.

➤ Right In **HANSJORG SCHAFER's**
The Untouchables **(1989)**, at the Unit 7
Gallery, London, the artist referred to
the social hierarchy of contemporary
Britain. The constructions included a
large sphere made from plates held
together with clothes pegs, and a
pyramid made entirely from champagne
glasses and tennis balls. A soundtrack
played 'The sun has got his hat on'.

▼ **ROBERT GOBER's** 1989 readymades at
the Paula Cooper Gallery, New York
➤ (below and opposite below), **were in fact
one-offs or hand-crafted artist products.**
In the room opposite below, **black silk-
screened *Male and Female Genital
Wallpaper* was hung with cast pewter
Drain insets. On a plinth in the centre
stood a *Bag of Donuts*, made from
paper, dough and rhoplex. A second
room** (below) **was covered in *Hanging
Man/Sleeping Man* wallpaper against
which rested bags of *Cat Litter*. The
room's focus was *Wedding Gown*.**

A sense of irony and knowing parody is present in the work of the Corsican-born artist Ange Leccia, the Belgian artist Wim Delvoye and the British artist Rob Kesseler.

◄ **ANGE LECCIA**'s 'arrangements' of readymades focus on the question of symmetry. They have featured cars, light fixtures, motorcycles, etc., placed face to face, as if engaged in intimate conversation. In *Arrangement 1990* (left), two bulldozers were parked outside the Art Gallery of New South Wales, Sydney. Inside the gallery was a further 'arrangement' of three rows of 21 empty boxes which had previously contained television sets but now contained only white protective styrofoam. On an adjacent wall a lightbox showed a slide of an explosion.

➤ In **WIM DELVOYE**'s *Senza Titoli (Untitled)* (1990) at the Museum of Contemporary Art, Ghent (right), a hand-painted image of a bejewelled cat stared out at rows of empty, mouse-sized rocking chairs made from clothes pegs.

▼ **ROB KESSELER** showed *Stable* (below), his ironic commentary on the market-ing of art and artists, at the Art/London '90 exhibition, held in the National Hall of Olympia. It consisted of three empty horseboxes made from pressboard. The first ('Clear Impression') had an orange rubber carpet underlay floor, on which sat four dark satin pillows displaying glass horseshoes. The floor of the central container ('Base Metal') was made from straw compressed by a steel rectangle with four horseshoe cutouts. On the green baize felt floor of the third box ('Fool's Gold') stood four mounds of coal on which were displayed four gilt horseshoes.

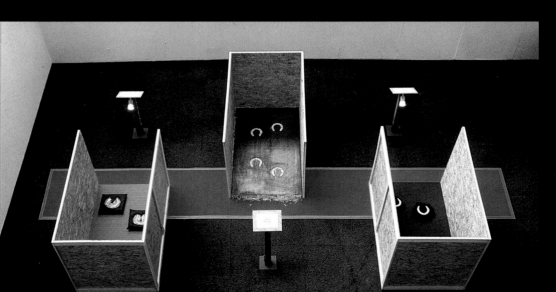

➤ Opposite **THOMAS LOCHER** is best known for his two-dimensional work dealing with the basic elements of language. In *Markierung und Etikettierung* (Marking and Labelling), his installation at the Tanja Grunert Gallery, Cologne, in 1989, the hard-edged furniture objects were carved with 450 sentences such as 'Am I being misled?' and 'How is this to be construed?' The sentences questioned not only the effectiveness of communication in general but the whole existence of the work itself.

★ JONI MABE'S ★
★ ★ WORLD FAMOUS
TRAVELING ELVIS MUSEUM ★

ZERO ONE GALLERY ★
7025 MELROSE AVE.
HOLLYWOOD, CA 90038
(213) 965-0459
GALLERY HOURS: TUES. - SAT. 11 - 6

★ DEC. 10 - JAN. 14 1989
Opening night DEC. 10 (SAT.) 8 - 11pm

SATISFACTION GUARANTEED

In these installations the artists have taken on the traditional role of curator, while simultaneously questioning the validity of the museum within the larger popular culture.

▲ The U.S. artist **JONI MABE**'s *Travelling Elvis Museum* (above) was shown at the Zero One Gallery, Hollywood, in 1989. It consisted of thousands of pieces of Elvis Presley memorabilia as well as specially created objects. A 'May-be Elvis Toenail', found by Mabe in the carpet at

Graceland (the Presley home and gravesite), was included among the exhibits. Visitors could buy a limited edition Elvis prayer rug, sachets of earth from Graceland, and surrealistic badges labelled 'Elvis's Hair', which contained actual human hair.

DANNY TISDALE's *Black Museum* of 1990 (above and below), shown at the Intar Gallery, P.S.1., New York, was a wry satire on the position of the Black American within the dominant white culture. Viewers passed through bead curtains into a 1970s hairsalon, complete with Afro combs, wigs, hair colours and straighteners, skin lighteners, etc. Advertising materials from the 1950s to the 1980s, including a stack of scrapbooks containing 'Black' magazines such as *Jet*, provided a commentary on the aspirations of African-Americans during that period.

Beaubourg, Paris. Did *Plight* exist as an art work only while at the d'Offay? Are the objects of the installation of curatorial value in themselves? Is a transformation of the Beuys idea without his hand still the same work of art?

To complicate matters, Beuys himself remade works so that they looked quite different. *Dernier espace avec introspecteur* (Last Space with 'Introspector'), for example, was first ▲ staged in 1964, then shown at the ▲ Anthony d'Offay Gallery (above centre),

▲ in 1982, and again at the Durand-Dessert, Gallery, Paris (above), in the same year. While the elements were essentially the same, the placement within the galleries was not, so they can be considered as separate installation works.

The works of David Hammons and Rasheed Araeen are critiques of Western culture and colonialism.

▲ **DAVID HAMMONS** deals with issues of race and considers his witty installations to be similar to jazz improvisations. He often arrives a few days prior to the opening of a work to take inspiration from the site, as he did with *Yo-Yo* (above), his contribution to the 1991 Carnegie International, at the Carnegie Museum of Art, Pittsburgh. First he placed cheap wallpaper on one wall. An adjacent wall was covered with smudges which he had made by throwing a basketball against it. The ball itself sat in the centre of the space inside a paint-mixing machine, which was activated periodically, causing the ball to gyrate. These motions were accompanied by music from a 'ghettoblaster'.

▼ The work of **RASHEED ARAEEN** often focuses on his position as an outsider – an Asian artist within Western culture. His two floor pieces at the Showroom Gallery, London, in 1988 satirized the work of Richard Long. The rectangle
▲ (below left) was composed of real bones; the circle (below) of empty wine bottles.

➤ **VICTOR SKERSIS** and **VADIM ZAKHAROV** (S/Z) belonged to the Aptart (Apartment Art) group, who produced performance art works and installation projects in the early 1980s in the USSR. Since 1984 Skersis has lived in the USA. S/Z reunited in 1990 to create a piece for The Work of Art in the Age of Perestroika exhibition at the Phyllis Kind Gallery, New York. Entitled *The Author/The Book*, it consisted of a faded black and white image, a shrouded empty chair and a clinically clean white table on which was placed a stainless steel medical pan (opposite). The work was intended to be part of Zakharov's ongoing exploration of Dostoevsky's novel *The Brothers Karamazov*.

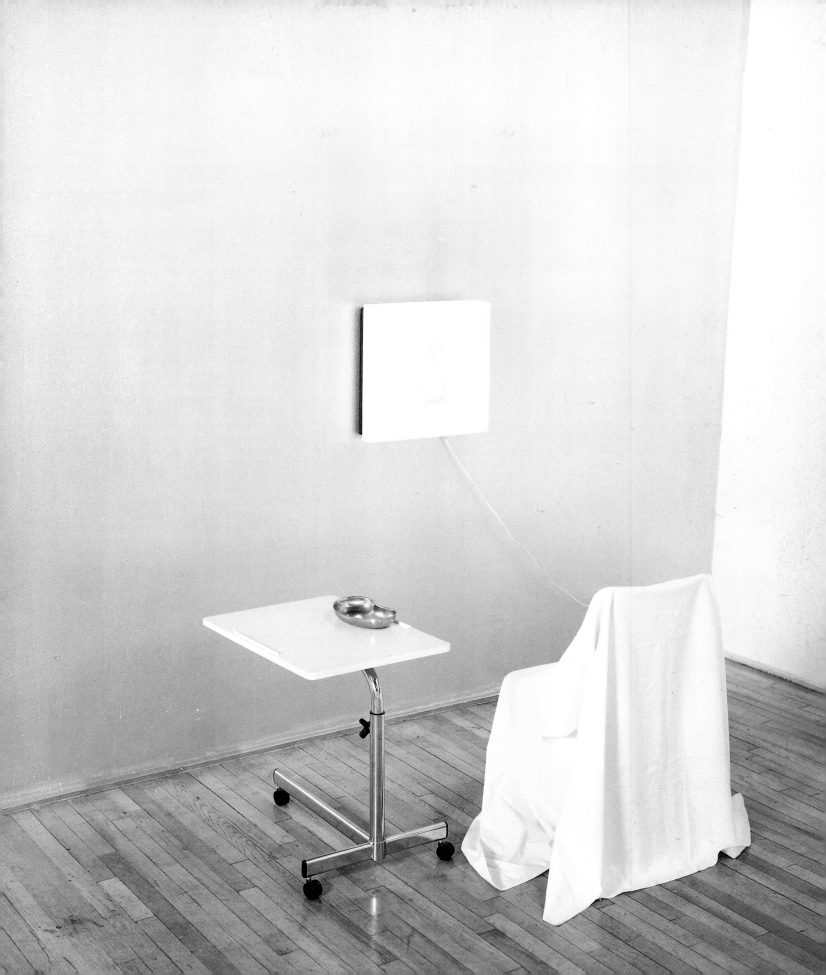

> **LOUISE LAWLER**'s contribution to the 1991 Carnegie International featured three interventions in the Carnegie Museum of Art, Pittsburgh, based on other pieces in the collection. All three commented on the position of the female artist within the art world/museum structure. *HAVING ATTAINED VISIBILITY AS WELL AS MANAGING TO CATCH THE EYE OF THE SPECTATOR...* consisted of a photographic image of a Warhol work, mounted near a painted script by Tony Di Spigna ('Squid in Its Own Ink'), and a glass paperweight. The work was installed in one of the main galleries.

◀ Multiples of mass-produced objects, or objects which intentionally appear to be mass produced, form the basis of **ALLAN McCOLLUM**'s installations. He cast hundreds of dinosaur bones from the Carnegie's Museum of Natural History collection for his *Lost Objects* (left), created for the 1991 Carnegie International. The enamel-covered concrete bones were placed on a central dais in the sculpture court. His *Plaster Surrogates* (left, centre) have been shown in various sites, installed in different formations. They consist of casts of pictures in frames, usually painted black, replicated hundreds of times in various sizes. Through them McCollum questions the value of the discrete handmade object.

▼ British artist **TONY CRAGG** assembled hundreds of fragments of coloured plastic to create a series of works in the early 1980s. Like other works by Cragg, *Riot* (below) could be dismantled and resited. It is shown here at the Hayward Gallery, London, in 1987.

▼ In *The Perfect Thought* (below), an exhibition of sculptural objects, the U.S. artist **JAMES LEE BYARS** combined past works to create a new installation. In the modernist space of the Art Museum at the University of California at Berkeley, Byars painted two gold leaf circles on the floor. The smaller was empty, while the larger (42 feet in diameter) held 23 separate works. Visitors were not allowed inside the circles but could view the work from the many internal levels provided by balconies and stairs.

➤ **SHERRIE LEVINE** has appropriated famous male artistic identities in order to criticize patriarchal systems from within. For *La Fortune (After Man Ray: 1-4)*, of 1991 (opposite), she installed four billiard tables in the Mary Boone Gallery in New York. They were functionless objects, with the balls placed identically on each table.

▼ **IMI KNOEBEL**'s *Raum 19* (Room 19) of 1968 (below) is a collection of assorted fibreboard stretchers and forms devoid of colour. The work has existed in many formats since its conception and initial installation. It has been presented in 'storage' form, spread throughout a museum, and most recently at the Dia Art Foundation in a compacted format that enhanced the theatricality of the work. Here the piece was lit only by daylight, but it has also been seen in artificial light at Galerie Heiner Friedrich in 1978. *Raum 19* exemplifies installation at its most flexible, commenting on the idiom's capability to represent its components in many guises.

British artist **MICHAEL LANDY**'s *Market*, at Building One, London, in 1990 (opposite), consisted of 'sculptures' made from stacked empty bread crates and artificial grass on metal frames. The fact that the turf displays were identical to those found in London street markets, and that the bread baskets still had a potential for use, questioned notions of display and the uniqueness of the art object.

➤ **IAN HAMILTON FINLAY**'s *Inter Artes et Naturam* (Between Art and Nature) was shown at the Victoria Miro Gallery, London, in 1988 (right). The title refers to a Puvis de Chavannes painting which places an orchard next to a wilderness. The trellis was constructed with irregular pieces of wood on the outside and with planed wood at the centre of the cross. The progression from wilderness to controlled space as the viewer entered into the work paralleled the juxtaposition of natural and manmade woodland environments in the Puvis painting.

▼ **MAGDALENA JETELOVA** was exiled from Czechoslovakia in 1985, before the fall of Communism. Her enormous chairs, stairs, and tables refer not only to the vast scale and monumentalism of Soviet art, but also to issues of dominance, control and oppression. Jetelova's two huge black tables at the Henry Moore Sculpture Trust Studio, Halifax, in 1990, slanted down into the space. The wood had been burnt to achieve the rich black colour (below).

The Catholic Church has long taught men and women to loathe their bodies and to fear their sexual natures. This particular vision of good and evil continues to bring suffering and even death. By holding medicine hostage to Catholic morality and withholding information which allows people to protect themselves and each other from acquiring the Human Immunodeficiency Virus, the Church seeks

"The truth is not in condoms or clean needles. These are lies ... good morality is good medicine."
John Cardinal O'Connor, First Vatican Conference on AIDS, 19

to punish all who do not share in its peculiar version of human experience and makes clear its preference for living saints and dead sinners. It is immoral to practice bad medicine. It is bad medicine to deny people information that can help end the AIDS crisis. Condoms and clean needles save lives as surely as the earth revolves around the sun. AIDS is caused by a virus and a virus has no morals.

SEXISM REARS ITS UNPROTECTED HEAD
MEN USE CONDOMS OR BEAT IT
AIDS KILLS WOMEN

These installations look at forms of social control: through voyeurism, education and sexuality.

◄ The work of the French artist **SOPHIE CALLE** (opposite) evolves from projects in which she acts as voyeur or detective. *The Blind* (1989), at the Fred Hoffman Gallery, Santa Monica, California, featured 23 sets of photographs of interviewees who had been blind from birth. Calle asked them to describe their idea of beauty. She then presented a text outlining their idea, a photograph of the idea, and a photograph of the person.

➤ **GROUP MATERIAL** (opposite below) is a New York collective that produces installations based on contemporary social issues. *Education and Democracy* (1988), at the Dia Art Foundation, New York, featured a simulated classroom. The images in this work addressed educational issues and looked at the role of art both as a seat of resistance and as a generator of harmful propaganda.

▼ **GENERAL IDEA** (A.A. Bronson, Felix Partz and Jorge Zontal) (below) produced The Public and Private Domains of the Miss General Idea Pavilion at the San Francisco Artspace in 1988. The works

featured included *The AIDS Poster Project* and *The AIDS Room from the Pavilion* (above). Both were based on a refiguration of Robert Indiana's iconic 1960s LOVE graphic.

▲ The **GRAN FURY** collective's installation at the 1990 Venice Biennale (above) was the focus of huge controversy. Originally banned, it was reinstated only when all the other artists in the Aperto section threatened to withdraw. The work took the form of three related billboards on the subject of AIDS (two shown here).

◄ **PETER ZIMMERMAN'S** elongations of what appeared to be ordinary empty cardboard boxes (left) seemed to have been casually left lying around on the floor of the Tanja Grunert Gallery, Cologne, in 1991. Their 'original contents' were barely discernible from the distorted outside lettering.

◄ *Fridge in Heaven* by **JOEL OTTERSON** (left) was installed in 1990 at the Daniel Buchholz Gallery, Cologne. In the centre of the gallery stood a customized chaise-longue on which the spectator could recline while watching the television positioned at the foot. It was also possible to obtain food and drink from a decorated refrigerator at the head. The walls were covered with posters of pop stars and film idols, as well as kitsch art scenes.

➤ **DAVID TREMLETT**'s installation of *Wall-Drawings* was made in 1991 at the Massimo Valsecchi Gallery, Milan. Six wall drawings occupied different locations in the space. Shown here (right) are a yellow drawing, on the left, and a dark brown drawing, on the right. Both connected the floor to the original frescoes above. There was also a small drawing above the door. The room was formerly part of a bank and the ceiling is by Donato Bramante.

▲ The Canadian-born artist **JESSICA STOCKHOLDER** showed *Where It Happened* (above) in 1990 at the American Fine Arts Gallery, New York.

Discrete objects with a history (a chest of drawers, newspapers, carpets) seemed randomly mixed with papier maché, styrofoam and sheetrock.

Paint was washed over parts of the work, and appeared to be the only unifying element, ordering the apparent chaos.

When things outside art come into the realm of art, are they legitimized by our tacit understanding and acceptance of the position of the fine art gallery?

▼ **MIKE KELLEY**'s use of soiled stuffed animals and blankets in a variety of tableaux suggests that this may not always be the case. In *Craft Morphology Flow Chart* (below), for the 1991 Carnegie International, the toys retained their power as objects and, despite Kelley's arrangements of them, remained firmly within the real world.

▲ **JESSICA DIAMOND** painted the walls of the San Francisco Artspace in 1990 for her 'Food for Thought' exhibition (above). Works in the exhibition included: *The Recipe: …* (1986/90) (in front of the sink); *Garlic* (1989) (above the sink); *Government Cheese with Stink* (1983/90); *T.V. Telepathy* (1989); *No Inside, No Outside* (1990); *Tijuana* (1988); *Those Who Dream and Do* ('coffee achievers') (1984); and *Elvis Alive* (1988/89).

Barriers, boundaries and the activities of contemporary American life feature ➤ in **CADY NOLAND**'s work. In *Office Filter* (1990) at the Touka Museum of Contemporary Art, Japan (opposite), she used poles to create a grill structure from which a flower-patterned blazer was suspended. The poles defined an arena in which office furniture and artefacts could be displayed.

In 1988, **HAIM STEINBACH** was part of a large group show at the World Financial Center, New York, addressing the question of the New Urban Landscape. For *Adirondack Tableau* (above), he placed a false wall of timber planks in the polished marble and glass area.

Cut into the wall was a window from which two handcarved owls peered out. A wooden seat, in front of the faux cabin, faced the connecting lobby area. The rustic materials contrasted with the expensive and cosmopolitan (international modernist) style.

ARCHITECTURE

Part of McLuhan's run-down of the implications of electronic media developments goes:

The telephone: **speech without walls.**

The phonograph: **music hall without walls.**

The photograph: **museum without walls.**

The electric light: **space without walls.**

The final dissolution of the gallery wall as physical barrier paved the way for its assertion as ideological support or screen. This is also seen in work outside the area of installation, for example in photographic work by Gönther Förg or Candida Höfer. Förg's facades of Italian buildings of the fascist period, and Höfer's interiors, reveal architecture not as innocent manipulation of spatial form, but as ideology made concrete.

From the sixties onwards, Dan Graham has been making work which confounds, through the use of glass, mirrors and video apparatus, our understanding of inside and outside. The physical aspects to this – being within/outside and seeing into/out of a space – are seen by Graham to parallel the processes of consciousness whereby we apprehend time and our presence within its flow. The mirror and the video playback represent, as it were, the different axes of consciousness, the synchronic and diachronic:

Mirrors reflect instantaneous time without duration . . . and they totally divorce our exterior behaviour from our inside consciousness - whereas video feedback does just the opposite, it relates the two in a kind of _durational time_ flow.[1]

Brian Hatton has compared Graham's 1966 magazine project, Homes for America, in which photographs of suburban housing evoked the serial structure and placement of Minimal sculpture, to Robert Smithson's Monuments of Passaic. In moving towards his formulation of the environment/gallery relationship as site/nonsite, Smithson had photographically documented industrial installations in New Jersey. (And again, think, too, of the water tower and grain silo photographs of Höfer's tutors, Bernd and Hilla Becher. In fact, not only in Höfer, but also in the work of their other pupils, Thomas Struth, Axel Hütte and Andreas Gursky, does one see the larger environment as richly coded.) Graham, though, is 'interested in the entropy of the suburbs not as a metonym for the cosmos, but as a communal – though empty – sign system, directing and limiting circuits of desire and exchanges of identity.'[2]

In 1973 a group of artists working in New York – Laurie Anderson, Tina Girouard, Suzanne Harris, Jene Highstein, Bernard Kirschenbaum, Richard Landry and Gordon Matta-Clark – developed a project around the notion of 'Anarchitecture'. Matta-Clark discussed the idea in an interview the following year.

Our thinking about anarchitecture was more elusive than doing pieces that would demonstrate an alternative attitude to buildings, or, rather to the attitudes that determine containerisation of usable space. We were thinking more about metaphoric voids, gaps, left-over spaces, places that were not developed. . . . For example, the places where you stop to tie your shoelaces, places that are just interruptions in your own daily movements.[3]

At the beginning of the decade, Matta-Clark had collaborated with Harris, Girouard and others in setting up and running the restaurant, 'Food', in New York's SoHo district. This and other projects by Matta-Clark at the time – piling up junk and roasting a pig under Brooklyn Bridge, for example – echo Acconci's sense of art as something which forms a community and calls it to a particular purpose. From 1971 until his death in 1978 Matta-Clark made a series of works which involved cutting into and transforming buildings. Dan Graham points out that in contrast to the Land Art and much environmentally concerned work of the period, Matta-Clark's work centred on the experience of urban existence:

'Nature' was an escape; political and cultural contradictions were not to be denied. By making his removals something like the spectacle of a demolition for casual pedestrians, the work could function as a kind of urban 'agit-prop', something like the acts of the Paris Situationalists, in 1968, who had seen their acts as public intrusions or 'cuts' into the seamless urban fabric.[4]

Dennis Adams's 'bus shelters' continue this strand of urban agit-prop, and, in their different ways, both the playful facades designed by the SITE group and Tadashi Kawamata's wooden constructions which ambivalently suggest simultaneous processes of development and decay extend the idea of deconstructing architectural norms. All these instances present architecture as something usable, something which comes and goes, its aspirations to permanence continually undermined. In the crevices of real-life dereliction, Charles Simonds builds his miniature ruins, and these, too, are abandoned to their fate. What remains, as we see, for example, in Rachel Whiteread's 'death mask' casts of domestic spaces and objects, is the historical and personal resonance of the site.

In the 1970s the French artist **JEAN-PIERRE RAYNAUD** developed his house into an installation like Kurt Schwitters's *Merzbau*, where the work started in one room and eventually took over the entire building. Almost every surface in Raynaud's house is covered in white tile with black grout; he even sleeps in a white tiled bed.

▲ Raynaud's ultimate transformation of an urban site was his proposal *La Tour Blanche* (1984), in which he suggested that an abandoned highrise in the immigrant neighbourhood of Les Minguettes near Lyons should be completely covered in tile and turned into a public work (left). The project has been accepted but has yet to be realized. *La Carte du Ciel*, at La Grande Arche in the new Parisian suburb of La Défense (below), features a huge outdoor grid made from white marble and black granite. The work is sited on the four patios at the summit of the arch, and is exposed to the daylight.

➤ **DANIEL BUREN** intervenes in architecture, introducing his 'stripes' on the sides of buildings or false walls. In 1989, at the Rath Museum in Geneva (right), Buren partially encased the building in a work entitled *Une enveloppe peut en cacher une autre* (One Container May Hide Another). The diagonal structure disrupted the normal view of the Museum and created a new temporary entrance. At the Serpentine Gallery, London, in 1987 (right below), Buren bisected the building on the north–south and east–west axis. The walls, with regular cut-out 'window' spaces, allowed a view of the building and its park site.

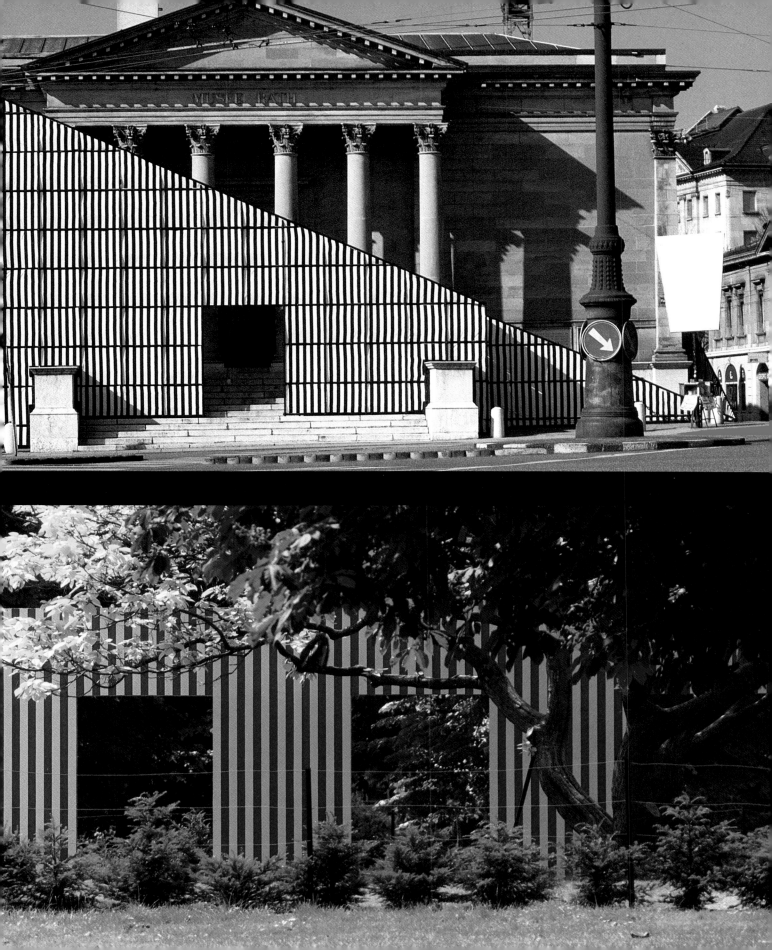

◀ **VITO ACCONCI**'s exploration of architectural form has extended to works like his 1988 *House of Cars 2* (left) in which he created an urban dwelling by cannibalizing six cars and then recombining them into a three-apartment structure. Wood and corrugated steel walls created separate functional living areas. The cars were coated a dull grey and a flickering neon sign read: 'Live out of this world'.

▶ *Sub-Urb* (left below), of 1983, was sited underground. It was a series of rooms made from wood and steel and roofed with Astroturf. The rooms were accessible by walking down the steps revealed by the opened panels. When the panels were closed, the underside formed an American flag.

▶ **SITE PROJECT**'s *Highway '86 –*
▼ *Processional* (opposite and below) was the winning entry for a transportation/communication pavilion and procession for the 1986 World Expo in Vancouver, Canada. A steel and concrete four-lane boulevard, it rose out of the sea and occupied the entire length of the central space. The surface was covered in cars, motorcycles, bicycles, boats, aeroplanes, etc., all painted the monochrome light grey of the surrounding concrete. *Highway '86* was conceived as a commentary on people's ambivalent relationship with technology in the 1980s – as leading either to utopia or to apocalypse.

The abuse of power has been the focus of **DENNIS ADAMS**'s work. His site-specific 'Bus Shelters' contain large photographs which replace advertising posters. *Bus Shelter IV* (right), installed in the Domplatz, Münster, Germany, during the trial of Klaus Barbie, showed photos of Barbie and his lawyer. In an earlier work (below) of 1980, *Shifting Cinema for a Red, White and Blue Movie*, at Miami University, Ohio, he used sound footage of Joseph McCarthy's HUAC hearings, which was back-projected onto a screen split by a wall. Two-thirds of the image could be seen in the red room – the blue room was blocked to visitors, but still visible. In an adjacent corridor a four-track tape could be heard of a female voice recollecting a lecture by McCarthy in which he announced his agenda.

DAN GRAHAM's 'Rooftop Urban Park Project' (1991-1993/94) at the Dia Centre for the Arts in New York (opposite, above and below) continued his investigations into the architecture of 'social' space. On the arts centre rooftop he placed a simple 36-foot square of glass. The steel-framed two-way reflective glass walls – often found in Graham's work – held an internal 10-foot cylinder with a door (above). The roof area included a café and a video room converted from a utility hut.

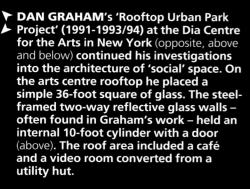

Deconstruction, alteration, revision, change... All these works are based on models that already exist.

➤ The Japanese artist **TADASHI KAWAMATA** is known for cladding buildings in readymade dereliction. In his construction on the Annely Juda Gallery in London in 1990 (right), planks protruded in and out of the windows. The artist hoped to suggest both demolition and renovation. In fact, this was the final installation at the gallery – it moved to a new location after Kawamata's exhibition.

◄ The Polish architect **DANIEL LIBESKIND's** *Line of Fire* (left) for the Centre d'Art Contemporain in Geneva in 1988 traced a path through the columns of the glazed building. A metal plate with a cut-out cross shape acted as a makeshift 'sight' and was placed at one end of the construction. Incisions through the top of the piece and along its length created a further line of sight and allowed views into its core, represented by drawings by the artist.

▲ *The Skin of the Earth* was an
◄ architectural project developed by the architect **RAOUL BUNSCHOTEN** and his collaborator Alain Chiaradia. It was originally exhibited during October 1990 in the House of Architects in Moscow. A 'dissolution' in fifteen parts (the same number as the former Soviet Union), it showed a house in a state of disintegration, with an uncertain identity. The 'domestic inventory' comprised fifteen objects cast in ferro-concrete laid out within the frame provided by the building. Shown here are Raoul Bunschoten's 'Tricycle and Overview' (left) and 'Bed & Night Table' (above).

In *Was Machen*? (What Is to Be Done?) the Italian artist **MARIO MERZ** displayed a neon sign over the platform of a railway station in former East Berlin ◄ (left). This work, dated 1990, stressed the range of possible developments after the imminent reunification of the two Germanys. The sign could be read both as a question and as an expression of indecision.

➤ *Noi giriamo intorno alle case o le case girano intorno a noi*? (Do We Circle the Houses or Do the Houses Circle Us?) (opposite) was based on one of Merz's familiar igloo shapes. It was shown at Chapelle St-Louis de la Sulpetrière, Paris, in 1987. Its 1977/85 date suggests its use as part of an earlier work. Merz often recombines elements to create a lineage throughout his work.

▼ The **ARC GROUP** build structures within buildings. The works shown here, *The Ark* (below) at Balls Pond Road, London, ➤ and *The Lighthouse* (right), at the Accademia d'Brera in Milan, were both made from wood and tissue paper. Their enormous scale emphasized the fragility of the materials.

Since the 1970s, the U.S. artist **CHARLES SIMONDS** has created the archaeological remains of an imaginary civilization, which he calls the Little People. He installs miniature architectural structures – resembling pueblo dwellings – in window sills or cracks in walls in New York's Lower East Side. Most of his more than 300 works, made from tiny, unbaked clay bricks,

have disintegrated or have been taken away as souvenirs. His permanent installation, *Dwelling* (above, left and right), was carved in 1981 into a brick wall in the basement of the Museum of Contemporary Art in Chicago.

▼ In *Portrait of an Unknown Person or Peter Carl Fabergé's Nightmare* (below), Soviet architects **ALEXANDER BRODSKY**

and **ILYA UTKIN** also seem to be offering a parable about a culture, but one with an enigmatic message. This installation and the work opposite were shown at the Ronald Feldman Gallery, New York, in 1991. *Forum de Mille*
➤ *Veritatis* (Forum of a Thousand Truths) featured 16 columns covered in xeroxed notes, sketches and tear-off phone numbers.

LOREN MADSEN's huge *Floating Cross* at Wright State University, Dayton, Ohio (left), was made from hundreds of bricks and steel wire. Madsen transformed what looked like walls into a floating, almost weightless construction which was suspended high above the spectator's head.

SIMON UNGERS' *Post and Beam (Umbau 1)* at the Sophia Ungers Gallery, Cologne (right), in 1991, replicated the top half of the gallery site on the floor. Two columns were marked at halfway point and everything above this line was replicated in reverse. The viewer, on entering this disorientating space, could walk on the floor and the ceiling at once.

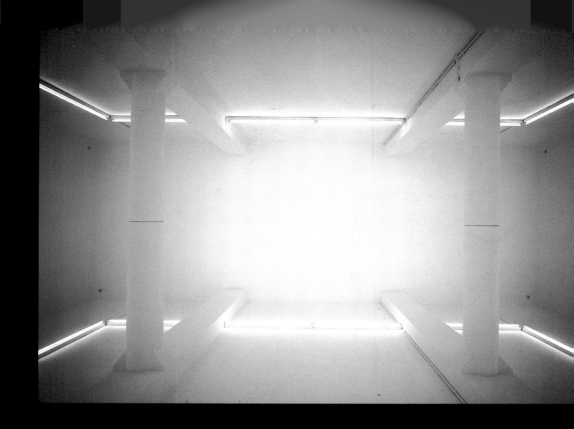

RICHARD ARTSCHWAGER has placed 'blps' on all manner of surfaces and sites to recontextualize them as works of art. The lozenge shape varies in size and media (paint, rubber, horsehair) but is always black and white. The 'blps' infiltrate exhibitions of his work, are placed on site (as, shown above, on the smoke stack of the Turtle Bay Steam Plant [Con Edison], Manhattan, *c.* 1970) or are exhibited in themselves (as, right, at the Clocktower, Institute for Art and Urban Resources, New York, 1978).

Architecture and illusion.

The British artist **RACHEL WHITEREAD** casts the space within objects in order to create a negative template. As part of her 1990 exhibition 'Ghost' (above), at the Chisenhale Gallery, London, she presented a large-scale cast of an entire room. The architectural details – fireplace, tiles, windows, cornice, wainscoting – were clearly visible. The artist intended the room to be a 'ghost' of the original.

➤ **PETER FISCHLI** and **DAVID WEISS** created the untitled work (left below) for the Doubletake exhibition at the Hayward Gallery, London, in 1992. It could be viewed only through a glass window set in a locked door, and appeared to be an ordinary storage or caretaker's room, but the highly realistic looking objects were in fact made from carved and painted polyurethane.

▼ **SIAH ARMAJANI** transformed the Max Protech Gallery, New York, in 1987-88 to create *Sacco & Vanzetti Reading Room No. 2* (below). In this installation the visitor necessarily became part of the work.

➤ **ARAKAWA/MADELINE GINS**'s *Reverse-Symmetry Transverse-Envelope Hall* (1988) (right) was part of a larger work, *Process in Question/Bridge of Reversible Destiny*, at the Seibu Museum, Karuizawa, Japan. A traditional Japanese tea room was replicated on the floor and ceiling.

The British artist Mark Currah and the German artist Eberhard Bosslet have both used the paraphernalia of modern bureaucracy to comment on the legal and functional aspects of society.

MARK CURRAH's *Temple* (above), of 1989, a lattice-work of standard lengths

of 2 foot by 1 inch wood, was suspended diagonally below the heating pipes of the Unit 7 Gallery's skylit roof. Starting at head height at one end, the structure dipped to a few feet above the ground at the other. The ends of the wooden struts were wrapped in pages from British law statutes which were tied on by wire – a makeshift construction acting as a metaphor for the Law itself. At the Karl Bornstein Gallery in Santa Monica, California (left), false brick-coloured plinths acted as a base for **EBERHARD BOSSLET**'s *Restrisiko II* (Residual Risk), in which a forest of metal poles pushed two empty filing cabinets up out of useful reach. Though it aspires to be functional, Bosslet's work is transparently unproductive.

➤ **VONG PHAOPHANIT**'s 1991 installation *Tok tem edean kep kin bo dai* (What Falls to the Ground but Cannot Be Eaten) at the Chisenhale Gallery, London (right), consisted of a monumental arched entrance inscribed with a Loatian text and a 'forest' of bamboo rods suspended from the ceiling. A central light source cast a shadow on the floor. The archway acted as an entrance as well as a framing device for viewing the bamboo.

▲ The German artist **THOMAS SCHUTTE**'s *Big Building* (above) was shown at the Marian Goodman Gallery, New York, in 1989. A series of ten plywood and cardboard constructions in the form of skeletal high-rise buildings, it offered a critique of modernism in architecture and looked forward to its demise. The panels are joined by wooden dowels covered in cardboard.

▼ To view **NAT GOODEN**'s untitled 1990 installation at Matt's Gallery, London (below), the spectator climbed a temporary staircase to a platform at the top of the gallery. A gallery-sized geometric grid had been placed from wall to wall. The grid was made from ordinary wooden doors which had been carved out to form a bowl-shaped cavity.

NOTES ON THE TEXT

FOREWORD

1 Goldberg, RoseLee, 'Space as Praxis', *Studio International* 190, no. 977 (September/October 1975): 130-35. This is a special issue of *Studio International* devoted to art and architecture. Several of the contributions, notably those by Germano Celant and Dan Graham, are relevant to a consideration of installation.

TOWARDS INSTALLATION

1 Broodthaers, Marcel, 'Gare au Défi: Pop Art, Jim Dine and the Influence of René Magritte' in Buchloh, Benjamin H.D. (ed.), *Broodthaers: Writings, Interviews, Photographs*, Cambridge, Mass., and London: MIT Press, 1988, p. 34.
2 Apollinaire, Guillaume, *Les Peintres cubistes*, in Chipp, Herschel B., *Theories of Modern Art*, Berkeley, Los Angeles and London: University of California Press, 1973, p. 246.
3 Duchamp, Marcel, in conversation with George Heard Hamilton, *Audio Arts* vol. 2, no. 4, 1975.
4 Glaser, Bruce, 'Questions to Stella and Judd', interview broadcast on WBAI-FM, New York, February 1964, edited by Lucy R. Lippard and published in *Art News*, September 1966. Reprinted in Battcock, Gregory (ed.), *Minimal Art: A Critical Anthology*, New York: E.P. Dutton, 1968, pp. 148-64. Quote p. 162.
5 O'Doherty, Brian, *Inside the White Cube: The Ideology of the Gallery Space*, Santa Monica and San Francisco: Lapis Press, 1986, p. 34.
6 *Ibid.*, p. 29.

7 *Ibid.*, p. 15.
8 Broodthaers, *op. cit.* at note 1 above, p. 34.
9 Kristeva, Julia, 'Word, Dialogue and Novel', in Toril Moi (ed.), *The Kristeva Reader*, Oxford: Blackwell, 1986, pp. 48-49.
10 In the 'First Proclamation of the Weimar Bauhaus', Gropius wrote:

Architects, painters and sculptors must recognize anew the composite character of a building as an entity. Only then will their work be imbued with the architectonic spirit which it has lost in 'salon art'... Let us create a *new guild of craftsmen*, without the class distinctions which raise an arrogant barrier between craftsman and artist. Together let us conceive and create the new building of the future, which will embrace architecture *and* sculpture *and* painting in one unity and which will rise one day toward heaven from the hands of a million workers like the crystal symbol of a new faith.

See Bayer, Herbert, Gropius, Ise, and Gropius, Walter (eds), *Bauhaus 1919-1928*, Boston: Charles T. Branford, 1959, p. 16.
11 *Ibid.*, p. 162.
12 Quoted in Buck-Morss, Susan, *The Dialectics of Seeing: Walter Benjamin and the Arcades Project*, Cambridge, Mass.: MIT Press, 1989, p. 83.
13 *Ibid.*, p. 85.
14 Tatlin, quoted in Gray, Camilla, *The Russian Experiment in Art*, London and New York: Thames and Hudson, 1971, revised edition 1986, p. 225.
15 Gabo, Naum, 'The Realistic Manifesto', in Chipp, *op. cit.* at note 2 above, p. 328.
16 Marinetti, F.T., 'The Founding and Manifesto of Futurism',

1909, in Apollonio, Umbro (ed.), *Futurist Manifestos*, London: Thames and Hudson, 1973, p. 22.
17 Marinetti, F.T., Settimelli, Emilio, and Corra, Bruno, 'The Futurist Synthetic Theatre', 1915, in Apollonio, *op. cit.* at note 16 above, p. 194.
18 See Elderfield, John, *Kurt Schwitters*, London and New York: Thames and Hudson, 1987, pp. 106-107 for a discussion of Schwitters's theory of the Merz-theatre.
19 Buchloh, Benjamin H.D., 'Beuys: The Twilight of the Idol', *Artforum* (January 1980): 39-40.
20 *Ibid.*, p. 41.
21 Judd, Donald, 'Specific Objects', *Arts Yearbook 8*, 1965, reprinted in Judd, Donald, *Complete Writings 1959-1975*, Halifax, Nova Scotia: The Press of the Nova Scotia College of Art and Design; New York: New York University Press, 1975.
22 Morris, Robert, 'Notes on Sculpture', *Artforum* (February and October 1966), reprinted in Battcock, *op. cit.* at note 4 above, pp. 222-35. Quote p. 226.
23 *Ibid.*, p. 233.
24 *Ibid.*
25 The term 'distributed sculpture' comes from Livingston, Jane, 'Barry Le Va: Distributional Sculpture', *Artforum* (November 1968): 50-54, reprinted in *The New Sculpture 1965-1975*, catalogue to the exhibition at the Whitney Museum of American Art, New York, 1990, pp. 118-20. In the article, Livingston sees Le Va's sculpture as closer to Cubist collage than environmental sculpture.
26 Kozloff, Max, 'In a Warehouse: An Attack on the Status of the Object', review of the exhibition '9 at Castelli',

Artforum (February 1969), reprinted in *The New Sculpture*, *op. cit.* at note 25 above, pp. 106-107. Quote p. 106.
27 Morris, Robert, 'Anti-Form', *Artforum* (April 1968), reprinted in *The New Sculpture*, *op. cit.* at note 25 above, pp. 100-101.
28 Robert Morris had, in fact, invited Joseph Beuys to participate in '9 at Castelli', an invitation which, for mainly practical reasons, was declined. See Joseph Beuys interviewed by Willoughby Sharp, *Artforum* (December 1969): 42-47.
29 Pincus-Witten, Robert, 'Richard Serra: Slow Information', in *Postminimalism into Maximalism: American Art 1966-1986*, reprinted in *The New Sculpture*, *op. cit.* at note 25 above, pp. 152-55. Quote p. 155.
30 Rosenberg, Harold, 'The American Action Painters', in *The Tradition of the New*, Chicago, 1982, p. 25.
31 For a discussion of this, see Douglas Crimp, 'On the Museum's Ruins', in Foster, Hal (ed.), *The Anti-Aesthetic: Essays on Postmodern Culture*, Seattle, Washington: Bay Press, 1983, pp. 43-56. Other essays in the book also bear interestingly upon the subject of installation.
32 Kozloff, *op. cit.* at note 26 above, p. 107.
33 Worner, Karl H., *Stockhausen: Life and Work*, London: Faber, 1973, p. 236.
34 Definitions of Situationist terms originally published in *Internationale Situationiste* No. 1, June 1958. Reprinted in Blazwick, Iwona (ed.), *An endless adventure... an endless passion... and endless banquet: A Situationist Scrapbook*, ICA London/Verso, 1989, p. 22.
35 Wollen, Peter, 'Bitter

Victory' in *An endless adventure*, *op. cit.* at note 34 above, p. 10.
36 Fried, Michael, 'Art and Objecthood', *Artforum* (June 1967). Reprinted in Battcock, Gregory (ed.), *Minimal Art: A Critical Anthology*, London: E.P. Dutton, 1968, pp. 116-47.
37 Lippard, Lucy R., *Six Years: the Dematerialization of the Art Object*, London: Studio Vista, 1973.
38 Jameson, Fredric, 'Postmodernism and Utopia' in *Utopia Post-Utopia: Configurations of Nature and Culture in Recent Sculpture and Photography*, catalogue published by ICA, Boston; Cambridge, Mass., and London: MIT Press, 1988, p.15.
39 *Ibid*.
40 Goldberg, RoseLee, 'Space as Praxis', *Studio International* 190, no. 977 (September/October 1975): 134.
41 Jameson, *op. cit.* at note 38 above, p. 25.
42 Miller, John, text of a contribution to the symposium, 'What Is Social History?', at the Grazer Kunstverein, 1990. Quoted in Germer, Stefan, 'Das Museum, die hohe und die niedrige Kunst', *Texte zur Kunst*, Autumn 1990, p. 34.
43 John Cage in conversation with William Furlong, *Audio Arts* vol. 6, nos 2/3, 1983.

SITE

1 Holt, Nancy, statement in 'Situation Esthetics: Impermanent Art and the Seventies Audience', *Artforum* (January 1980): 26.
2 Smithson's table appeared in a number of places, including as a footnote to his essay on *The Spiral Jetty*, reprinted in Holt, Nancy (ed.), *The Writings of Robert Smithson*, New York University Press, 1979.
3 de Maria, Walter, 'The Lightning Field: Some Facts, Notes, Data, Information, Statistics and Statements', *Artforum* (April 1980): 58.
4 Cornwell, Regina, 'Landstrikes', *Artscribe* (Summer 1991): 24.
5 Smithson, Robert, 'Fragments of an Interview with P.A. Norvell, April 1969', in Lippard, Lucy, *Six Years: The Dematerialization of the Art Object*, London: Studio Vista, 1973, p. 87.
6 Smithson, Robert, 'A Sedimentation of the Mind: Earth Projects', *Artforum* (September 1968): 44-50.
7 Acconci, Vito, in 'Situation Esthetics', *op. cit.* at note 1 above, p. 22.

MEDIA

1 Moholy-Nagy, László, 'A New Instrument of Vision', 1933, reprinted in Passuth, Krisztina, *Moholy-Nagy*, London and New York: Thames and Hudson, 1987, p. 326.
2 McLuhan, Marshall, *Understanding Media*, Chicago, Ill.: Sphere, 1967, p. 301.
3 Cornwell, Regina, 'Where is the Window?', *Artscribe* (January/February 1991): 54.
4 Morgana, Aimee, in conversation with Michael Archer on 'Issues and Debates', *Audio Arts* vol. 11, nos 3 & 4, 1991.

MUSEUM

1 See *Richard Hamilton*, catalogue to Richard Hamilton's retrospective at the Tate Gallery, London, 1992, p. 151.
2 Baumgarten is only one of a number of artists who use anthropological data. For a consideration of his work and that of Nikolaus Lang, Anne and Patrick Poirier, and Christian Boltanski, see Schneider, Arnd, 'The Art Diviners', *Anthropology Today* 9, no. 2 (April 1993): 3-9.
3 See on this point the catalogue to the 1991 Carnegie International, published by The Carnegie Museum of Art, Pittsburgh, and Rizzoli, New York.
4 Broodthaers, Marcel, in an interview with Johannes Cladders, *INK-Dokumentation 4*, Zurich, 1979, quoted in Rainer Borgemeister, '*Section des Figures*: The Eagle from the Oligocene to the Present', in Buchloh, Benjamin, (ed.), *Broodthaers: Writings, Interviews, Photographs*, Cambridge, Mass., and London: MIT Press, 1988, pp. 135-51. Quote pp. 146-47.
5 Asher, Michael, quoted in Ann Rorimer, 'Michael Asher: Recent Work', *Artforum* (April 1980): 49.

ARCHITECTURE

1 Dan Graham, quoted in Goldberg, RoseLee, 'Space as Praxis', *Studio International* 190, no. 977 (September/October 1975): 130-35. Quote p. 134.
2 Hatton, Brian, 'Dan Graham: Present Continuous', *Artscribe* (November/December 1991): 67.
3 Matta-Clark, Gordon, interview with Liza Bear, 1974, reprinted in *Gordon Matta-Clark*, catalogue to the exhibition at IVAM, Valencia, 1993, p. 375.
4 Graham, Dan, 'Gordon Matta-Clark', in *ibid*, p. 378.

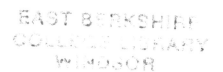

CHRONOLOGY

1879-1905
Hauterives, France: Ferdinand Cheval builds his 'Palais Idéal', a folly made from stones and shells

1896
Paris: *Ubu Roi* by Alfred Jarry; set designed by Jarry, Pierre Bonnard, Edouard Vuillard, Henri de Toulouse-Lautrec and Paul Sérusier; marks beginning of collaborations between theatre and art

1909
Paris: Filippo Tommaso Marinetti publishes the *Manifesto of Futurism* and presents his play *Roi Bombance*

1912-23
New York: Marcel Duchamp, *Large Glass*

1913
New York: Armory Show; 1600 works housed in a specially designed environment of octagonal rooms with open corners

Marcel Duchamp devises first 'readymade', a bicycle wheel mounted on a kitchen stool

1914
London and Milan: First performances of *Brutismo* by Russolo, combining noises from daily life in acoustic composition

1916
Zurich: Opening of Cabaret Voltaire, initiated by Hans Arp, Hugo Ball, Richard Huelsenbeck and Tristan Tzara, who adopt the name 'Dada'

1918
Tristan Tzara publishes *Dada Manifesto*

1919
Moscow: Monument to the Third International by Vladimir Tatlin

commissioned by the Department of Fine Arts (IZO)

Walter Gropius founds the Bauhaus in Weimar, moves to Dessau in 1925 and closes in 1933

1920
Berlin: Burchard Gallery, First International Dada Fair combining provocative theatre and visual art

Johannes Baader presents his installation *Das Grosse Plasto-Dio-Dada-Drama 'Deutschlands Grosse und Untergang'* (The Great Plasto-Dio-Dada-Drama 'Germany's Greatness and Downfall')

Hanover, Germany: Kurt Schwitters begins first *Merzbau* or K de E, *Kathedrale des erotischen Elends* (Cathedral of Erotic Woes)

First showing of *The Cabinet of Dr Caligari*, a film by Robert Wiene, designed by Hermann Warm

1921-22
Moscow: Founding of Constructivism

Beginning of Bauhaus Theatre

1922
Stuttgart, Germany: First performance of *Triadic Ballet* by Oskar Schlemmer

1923
First exhibition of the 'Proun' environment by El Lissitzky

1924
Vienna: 'International Exhibition of New Theatre Techniques' organized at the Konzerthaus by Frederick Kiesler. Collaborators include Ferdinand Léger, Vsevolod Meyerhold, Max Reinhardt, Oskar Schlemmer and Alexander Vesnin. Features Kiesler's 'Space Stage'.

André Breton publishes first *Surrealist Manifesto*

1925
Paris: *City of Space* by Frederick Kiesler at the 'Exposition Internationale des Arts Décoratifs et Industrielles Modernes'

Paris: 'Exposition, la Peinture Surréaliste' at Galerie Pierre

1927
Paris: Marcel Duchamp creates *Porte, 11, Rue Larrey*

1929
New York: Opening of the Museum of Modern Art

Barcelona: International Exhibition includes German pavilion by Mies van der Rohe

1930
Woodstock, New York: Clarence Schmidt, 'Environment'

1932
New York: First Exhibition of Surrealist Art in the United States shown at the Julien Levy Gallery

1932-33
Alberto Giacometti, *The Palace at 4 a.m.*

1933
North Carolina: Founding of Black Mountain College, directed by John Price

1935-38
Tirgu-Jiu, Romania: Sculptural environment by Constantin Brancusi including *Gate of the Kiss*, *Table of Silence* and *Endless Column*

1936
New York: 'Fantastic Art, Dada,

Surrealism' exhibition at the Museum of Modern Art

1938
Paris: 'International Exhibition of Surrealism', organized by Duchamp; includes artists such as Salvador Dalí, Max Ernst and André Masson; features Marcel Duchamp's environment *1200 Bags of Coal*

1939
New York: Opening of the Solomon R. Guggenheim Foundation Museum of Non-Objective Painting, later to become the Solomon R. Guggenheim Museum

New York: Arrival of the first wave of European avant-garde artists fleeing the war in Europe

1941
New York: Peggy Guggenheim's Gallery, Art of This Century, opens in New York, its design a pioneering example of environment art

Paris: Marcel Duchamp completes his own museum in miniature, *La Boîte en valise*

1942
New York: Marcel Duchamp, *Mile of String* (installation), at the first 'Papers of Surrealism' exhibition, 551 Madison Avenue

1946
Buenos Aires: Lucio Fontana publishes *White Manifesto*

1946-66
New York: Marcel Duchamp, 'Etant Donnés' (environment) [Moved to Philadelphia Museum of Art in 1969]

1947
Milan: First Spatialist Manifesto, composed by Lucio Fontana, Giorgio

Kaisserlian, Beniamino Joppolo and Milena Milano, focusing on the need for an abstract art which addressed space and time

1948-49
Milan: Lucio Fontana exhibits first *Ambiente Spaziale* at Galleria del Naviglio

Woodstock, New York: Clarence Schmidt, *House on Ohayo Mountain* (environmental work)

1951
Brazil: First Sao Paulo Bienale

1952
London: Independents' Group (IG) founded at the Institute of Contemporary Arts. Members include Lawrence Alloway, Reyner Banham, Richard Hamilton, Eduardo Paolozzi and Alison and Peter Smithson

North Carolina: Event at Black Mountain College. Includes work by John Cage, Merce Cunningham, Charles Olsen and Robert Rauschenberg

Woodstock, New York: First recital of John Cage's *4'33"*, the first silent composition

1953
London: 'A Parallel of Art and Life - Man, Machine and Motion' exhibition at the I.C.A., with the collaborations of Nigel Henderson, Eduardo Paolozzi and Peter and Alison Smithson

1954
Paris: Wolf Vostell realizes the first of his *Décollages*

1955
Kassel, Germany: First 'Documenta' exhibition

North Carolina: *Minutiae* performance at Black Mountain College with sets by Robert

Rauschenberg, dance by Merce Cunningham and music by John Cage

1956
London: 'This Is Tomorrow' exhibition at the Whitechapel Gallery, with the participation of Richard Hamilton, Eduardo Paolozzi and members of the IG. Emergence of key issues concerning Pop Art and popular culture

1957
Milan: Piero Manzoni makes the first *Achromes*

Düsseldorf: Founding of Gruppe Zero

Vienna: Founding of 'O M Theatre' (Orgien Mysterien Theater) by Hermann Nitsch

New York: Leo Castelli Gallery opens

Paris: Gaston Bachelard publishes *Poétique de l'espace*

Paris: Roland Barthes publishes *Mythologies*

1958
Paris: Christo makes first wrapped objects *(empaquetages)*

New Brunswick, N.J.: First Happenings, by George Segal, Claes Oldenburg and Allan Kaprow, held at Oldenburg's farm

Paris: Yves Klein exhibits *Le Vide* (The Void) at the Galerie Iris Clert and performs the first of his *Pinceaux vivants*, later to be termed *Anthropometries*

New York: Mark Rothko begins *Four Seasons*, a series of mural paintings for Mies van der Rohe's Seagram building, in a room designed by Philip Johnson

Germany: Joseph Beuys begins *Plight*, last installed at the Anthony d'Offay Gallery, London, in 1985

1959
New York: Allan Kaprow, *18 Happenings in 6 Parts*, at the Reuben Gallery

New York: 'The Burning Building' exhibition by Red Grooms, at the Reuben Gallery

New York: Opening of the Solomon R. Guggenheim Museum in the building designed by Frank Lloyd Wright

Los Angeles: Ed Kienholz, *Concept-Tableaux*

1960
New York: Jean Tinguely, *Homage to New York*, at The Museum of Modern Art

New York: Jim Dine, *Car Crash*, at the Reuben Gallery

Paris: Arman, 'Manifestation of Garbage' exhibition, at the Iris Clert Gallery

New York: Robert Whitman, *The American Moon* (performance), at the Reuben Gallery

1961
Paris: Happening takes place at the U.S. Embassy, with the participation of Jasper Johns, Robert Rauschenberg, Niki de Saint-Phalle and Jean Tinguely

The term 'Concept Art' is coined by Henry Flynt

New York: Ed Kienholz, *Roxy's*, at the Dwan Gallery

Piero Manzoni makes his first 'Magic Base', on which he signs and exhibits members of the audience. At Herning Kunstmuseum in Denmark he exhibits *Base of the World*

New York: George Segal exhibits *Man at a Table*, the first of his tableaux modelled on the human body

Paris: 'Forty Degrees Above Dada' exhibition, curated by Pierre Restany, at Galerie J.

New York: 'The Art of Assemblage' exhibition, curated by William C. Seitz, at The Museum of Modern Art

New York: 'Environments, Situations, Places' exhibition, including work by Jim Dine and Claes Oldenburg, at the Martha Jackson Gallery

1961/65
New York: Claes Oldenburg, *Store* (installation) and *Store Days* (performances)

1962
Paris: Ben (Vautier) sells himself as a 'Living Sculpture'

New York: 'The New Realists' exhibition, at the Sidney Janis Gallery

Wiesbaden, Germany: Fluxus International Festspiele festival. Includes work by Joseph Beuys, George Brecht, Robert Filiou, On Kawara, George Maciunas, Yoko Ono, Nam June Paik and Wolf Vostell

Andy Warhol, *200 Campbell Soup Cans*

1962/81
Rome: Luciano Fabro, *Habitat* (installation), at Galleria Mario Peroni

1963
New York: Hans Haacke begins his *Water Plus Wind Sculptures*

Wuppertal, Germany: Nam June Paik installation with prepared pianos, noise machines, televisions; Paik creates first video sculptures at the Galerie Parnass

Cologne, Germany: Joseph Beuys, his first use of fat as a substance during a lecture

1964

New York: Andy Warhol, *Brillo Boxes*

New York: Carolee Schneeman, *Meat Joy* (performance), at Judson Memorial Church

New York: Robert Morris and Carolee Schneeman, *Site* (action)

Kassel, Germany: Documenta 3, 'Museum of the 100 Days'

1965

Wuppertal, Germany: Joseph Beuys, *Twenty-four Hours* (Happening)

New York: Ed Kienholz, *The Beanery*, installed permanently at the Stedelijk Museum, Amsterdam

Vienna: Günther Brus and Rudolph Schwarzkogler begin their 'self-mutilations'

Stockholm: 'Inner and Outer Space' exhibition, organized by Pontus Hulten, at the Moderna Museet

1966

First earthworks by Richard Long, Robert Morris and Robert Smithson

Turin: Mario Merz begins *Fibonacci* series

Paris: Daniel Buren makes first striped paintings

New York: 'Nine Evenings of Theatre and Engineering'. Includes work by John Cage, Lucinda Childs, Oyvind Fahlstrom, Deborah Hay, Yvonne Rainer, Robert Rauschenberg, David Tudor and Robert Whitman. At the Armory

New York: 'Primary Structures' exhibition at the Jewish Museum, curated by Kynaston McShine, defines Minimalism as a movement. Participating artists include Carl Andre, Dan Flavin and Robert Morris. Includes Andre's seminal work *Lever*

Beginning of Body Art with Vito Acconci and Bruce Nauman

California: James Turrell makes his first light work, a projection piece called *Proto-Afrum*

1967

New York: Claes Oldenburg installs *Invisible Sculpture* behind the Metropolitan Museum of Art by digging and refilling a trench

Genoa, Italy: 'Arte Povera' exhibition with Alighiero Boetti, Luciano Fabro, Jannis Kounellis and Giulio Paoline, at Galleria La Bertesca

Paris: Daniel Buren, *Manifestation III* (installation), at Palais des Arts Décoratifs

New York: 'Projects for Macro-Sculpture' exhibition, at Richard Feigen Gallery

London: Gilbert & George call themselves 'The Human Sculptures' and proclaim that everything they do is sculpture

New York: Sol LeWitt, *Series A* (installation), at the Dwan Gallery

Turin: Michelangelo Pistoletto, *Venus degli Stracci* (Venus of the Rags), at Galleria Gian Enzo Sperone

Lanarkshire, Scotland: Ian Hamilton-Finlay begins his Sculpture Garden

New York: 'West Wall' exhibition by William Anastasi, at the Dwan Gallery

New York: Richard Artschwager develops the Blp

Washington, D.C.: 'Scale as Content: Ronald Bladen, Barnett Newman, Tony Smith' exhibition, at the Corcoran Gallery

New York: Paul Thek, *The Tomb - Death of a Hippie*, at the Stable Gallery

New York: Eva Hesse, *Repetition 19, First Version* (installation)

Robert Smithson publishes *Towards the Development of an Air Terminal Site*

New York: Hans Haacke, *Sky Line,* in Central Park

Joseph Kosuth publishes *Art as Idea as Idea*

New York: Opening Exhibition: 'Normal Art', organized by Joseph Kosuth, at the Lannis Museum of Normal Art

1968

New York: James Lee Byars sends a mile of gold thread into space via helium balloons, at the CBS Plaza, 53rd Street

Amalfi, Italy: 'Arte Povera, Azione Povera' exhibition, organized by Germano Celant, at Arsenale dell' Antica Repubblica

Robert Irwin and James Turrell undertake research on perception with Dr Edward Wortz

Kassel, Germany: Documenta 4

New York: Seth Siegelaub organizes first exhibition (by Douglas Hüebler) in catalogue form only

1969

James Turrell and Sam Francis make a series of airborne works with clouds and aeroplanes over Pasadena, California

Ithaca, New York: Robert Smithson first exhibits his *Nonsites* at Cornell University

New York: Vito Acconci, *Twelve Pictures* (performance)

New York: 'Anti-Form' exhibition, organized by Robert Morris. Includes work by Raphael Ferrer, Eva Hesse,

Barry Le Va, Bruce Nauman, Claes Oldenburg, Alan Saret, Robert Smithson and Keith Sonnier. Richard Serra presents *Casting* at the Leo Castelli Warehouse

New York: Establishment of Art Worker's Coalition (AWC) at the School of Visual Arts

New York: Robert Morris, *Continuous Project Altered Daily*

Little Bay, Sydney, Australia: Christo, *Wrapped Coast: One Million Square Feet*

Seattle, Washington: '557, 087' exhibition, organized by Lucy Lippard at the Seattle Art Museum. Includes work by Michael Asher, John Baldessari, Daniel Buren, Hanne Darboven, On Kawara, Joseph Kosuth and Sol LeWitt

New York: January Show, organized by Seth Siegelaub

New York: Lothar Baumgarten, *Terra Incognita* [also 1974, 1985, 1987, 1988]

New York: Eva Hesse, *Contingent* (installation)

Ithaca, New York: 'Earth Art' exhibition at Cornell University, showing work by artists concerned with process and anti-form. Includes work by Jan Dibbets, Hans Haacke, Richard Long, Robert Morris, Dennis Oppenheim and Robert Smithson

New York: 'Anti-Illusion: Procedures/Materials' exhibition, at the Whitney Museum of American Art

Rome: Jannis Kounellis, *Cavalli* (Horses), at Galleria L'Attico

Berne, Switzerland: 'When Attitudes Become Form' exhibition, curated by Harald Szeeman, at the Kunsthalle

Düsseldorf: 'The Ghost of James Lee Byars' exhibition, at the Kunsthalle

London: Gilbert & George present their first 'singing sculpture', *Underneath the Arches*

Berne, Switzerland: 'Plans and Projects as Art' exhibition, at the Kunsthalle

1969-70

Virgin River Mesa, Nevada: Michael Heizer, *Double Negative*

1969-85

Amsterdam: Lothar Baumgarten, *Tierra de los perros mudos* (Land of the mute dogs), at the Stedelijk Museum

1970

Los Angeles: Robert Barry exhibits a closed Art Gallery

London: 'Idea Structures' exhibition, organized by Charles Harrison with the participation of Art & Language, Robert Barry, Mel Bochner, Daniel Buren and Jan Dibbets, at Camden Central Library

Kent State, Ohio: Robert Smithson, *Partially Buried Woodshed* (earthwork)

New York: Yvonne Rainer, *Grand Union Dreams* (performance)

Osaka, Japan: Andy Warhol, *Daisy Fountain* (installation), at the United States Pavilion at Expo 70

New York: Dennis Oppenheim, *Parallel Stress* (performance)

Great Salt Lake, Utah: Robert Smithson, *Spiral Jetty*

Turin: 'Conceptual Art - Arte Povera - Land Art' exhibition, organized by Germano Celant at Galleria Civica d'Arte Moderna

1970-72

King City, Ontario: Richard Serra, *Shift*

1971

Santa Ana, California: Chris Burden presents *Shoot*, in which he maims his arm with a .22 pistol, at F Space

New York: Institute for Contemporary Art founded by Alanna Heiss

Salt Lake City, Utah: Gianni Pettena, *Clay House*

Santpoort-Velsen, Holland: Robert Morris, *Observatory*, at Sonsbeek Exhibition

Houston, Texas: Opening of Rothko Chapel

1972

Kassel, Germany: Documenta 5: 'Individual Myths - Parallel Picture Worlds' exhibition, organized by Konrad Fischer and Klaus Hohnef. Marcel Broodthaers presents his 'Musée d'Art Moderne, Département des Aigles'; Joseph Beuys's contribution comprises an office of information for the 'Organization for Direct Democracy through Referendum'

London: 'And for Today, Nothing', two-week action by Stuart Brisley at Gallery House

Düsseldorf: Joseph Beuys is dismissed from his teaching post at the Academy of Arts

The Bronx, New York: Gordon Matta-Clark, *Threshole*

London: Founding of Nice Style, the world's first Pose Band (Ron Carra, Bruce McLean, Paul Richards), which presents 999 pose pieces in self-proclaimed retrospective at Tate Gallery

New York: Vito Acconci, *Seedbed*, at the Sonnabend Gallery

1972-76

Marin County, California: Christo, *Running Fence*

1973

Genoa, Italy: Gordon Matta-Clark, *A. W. Hole House*

1973-76

Near Lucin, Utah: Nancy Holt, *Sun Tunnels*

1974

Near Flagstaff, Arizona: James Turrell begins *Roden Crater* project

Darmstadt, Germany: Walter de Maria, *The Large Earth Room*, at the Hessisches Landesmuseum

Amarillo, Texas: Ant Farm, *Cadillac Ranch*

New York: Dan Graham, *Present Continuous Past(s)* (video installation), at John Gibson Gallery

Philadelphia: Robert Morris, *Philadelphia Labyrinth* (installation), at the Institute of Contemporary Art

1974-77

Quemado, New Mexico: Walter de Maria, *Lightning Field*

1974-90

New York: Arakawa and Madeline Gins, *The Process in Question/Bridge of Reversible Destiny* (construction), at the Ronald Feldman Gallery

1975

Turin: Michelangelo Pistoletto, *Rooms*, at Galleria Christian Stein

Paris: Gordon Matta-Clark, *Conical Intersect*

Paris: Marcel Broodthaers, *La Salle blanche* (installation), at the Centre National d'Art Contemporain

London: Founding of the ACME Gallery by David Panton and Jonathan Harvey

1976

Brian O'Doherty (the Irish-born artist Patrick Ireland) publishes his essay *Inside the White Cube* in *Artforum*

New York: Installation on 3 floors by Michael Asher at the Institute for Art and Urban Resources, The Clocktower

New York: P.S.1 Museum opens, 'Rooms' exhibition

Piazza San Marco, Venice: Ha Schult, *6:00 A.M.*, an action/ installation involving 15,000 kg of paper

Venice: Joseph Beuys presents his installation *Tramway-Tramstop* as part of the 'Ambiente Art' exhibition at the Biennale

1977

Hartford, Conn.: Carl Andre *Stone Field Sculpture*, at the Joseloff Gallery

Kassel, Germany: Documenta 6: 'Art and Media'

London: Ting Theatre of Mistakes (founded 1974), *A Waterfall* (performance), at Hayward Gallery

1977-82

Eindhoven, The Netherlands: Lothar Baumgarten, *Die Namen der Baüme*

1977-85

Berne, Switzerland: Lothar Baumgarten, *Eldorado*, at the Kunsthalle

1978

New York: Mary Miss, *Perimeters, Pavilions, Decoys* (installation), exhibited at Nassau County Museum

London: Ron Haselden, *Working 12 Days*, shown at the Acme Gallery

1979

New York: Judy Chicago, *The Dinner Party*, at the Brooklyn Museum

Chicago: Art Institute of Chicago, 73rd American exhibition, curated by

James A. Speyer. Michael Asher removes the statue of George Washington from the entrance of the Institute and replaces it in Gallery 219 as part of his installation

1980

New York: Alice Maycock, *Large Scale Dis/Integration of Microelectric Memories (A Newly Revised Shanty Town)*, in Battery Park

Berlin: Büro Berlin, an experimental art space, is founded by Hermann Pitz, Fritz Rahmann and Raimund Kummer

Chicago: 'Vito Acconci: A Retrospective 1969 to 1980', at the Museum of Contemporary Art

London: Founding of Station House Opera, a performance group whose members are Julian Maynard-Smith, Miranda Payne and Alison Urquhart

Lake Placid, New York: Richard Fleischner, *Fence-Covered Fence* (environmental artwork)

1980-82

New York: Jenny Holzer, *The Living Series*

1981

Cologne: 'Westkunst' exhibition, curated by Kaspar König

Federal Plaza, New York: Richard Serra, *Tilted Arc* (sculpture)

Philadelphia: 'Machineworks: Vito Acconci, Alice Aycock, Dennis Oppenheim' exhibition, at the Institute of Contemporary Art

Los Angeles: 'Seventeen Artists in the Sixties - The Museum as Site: Sixteen Projects' exhibition, at the Los Angeles County Museum of Art

1982

Kassel, Germany: Documenta 7, curated by Rudi H. Fuchs, with the participation of 178 artists. Joseph

Beuys presents his interactive artwork *Aktion 7000 Eichen* (Action 7000 Oaks)

Pittsburgh: Mattress Factory, an exhibition space dedicated only to installation art, is founded by Barbara Luderowski

London: Opening of Matt's Gallery by Robin Klassnik

Pittsburgh: First Carnegie International at the Carnegie Museum of Art

Berlin: 'Zeitgeist' exhibition

Times Square, New York: Public showing of *Truisms* by Jenny Holzer

1983

Biscayne Bay, Florida: Christo, *Surrounded Islands* project

London: 'Scenes and Conventions - Artists' Architecture' exhibition, at the Institute of Contemporary Arts

1984

Sydney: Australian Biennial: 'Private Symbol: Social Metaphor', organized by Leon Paroissien. Includes the work of 63 artists

Washington D.C.: 'Content: A Contemporary Focus 1974-84', exhibition of the work of 137 artists, curated by Howard Fox, Miranda McClintic and Phyllis Rosenzweig. At the Smithsonian Institution

St Louis, Missouri: Alice Aycock, *The Hundred Small Rooms* (installation)

New York: 'Difference: On Representation and Sexuality' exhibition, curated by Kate Linker and Jane Weinstock. Includes work by Judith Barry, Dara Birnbaum, Barbara Kruger and Sherrie Levine. At the New Museum of Contemporary Art

1985

Los Angeles: 'The Artist as Social

Designer: Aspects of Urban Art' exhibition, at the Los Angeles Museum of Art

New York and Barcelona: Antoni Miralda, *Honeymoon Project* (completed in 1992)

Vienna: 'Kunst mit Eigensinn' (Obstinate Art) exhibition, at the Museum Moderner Kunst

New York: 'The Art of Memory/The Loss of History' exhibition, at The New Museum

Berlin: Opening of 'Ruine der Künste', a project space for site-specific works by Wolf Kahlen

1986

Ghent, Belgium: 'Chambres d'amis', exhibition of 50 installations in domestic locations in the city, curated by Jan Hoet. Includes work by Luciano Fabro, Joseph Kosuth, Mario Merz, Maria Nordmann, Jan Vercruysse

London: Hayward Gallery, 'Falls the Shadow', Hayward Annual exhibition, curated by Jon B. Thompson and Barry Barker. Includes work by Lothar Baumgarten, Marcel Broodthaers, Luciano Fabro, Jannis Kounellis and Wolfgang Laib

Barcelona: 'Art and Its Double' exhibition, curated by Dan Cameron, at the Centre Cultural de la Fundacio Caja de Pensions

California: 'Sitings' exhibition, curated by Hugh M. Davies and Ronald J. Onorato. Includes work by Alice Aycock, Richard Fleischner, Mary Miss and George Trakas. At La Jolla Museum of Contemporary Art

London: Opening of Unit 7 Gallery, dedicated to installation art

New York: 'Arts and Leisure' exhibition, curated by Group Material, at The Kitchen

Cologne: 'Europa - Amerika', an exhibition of the work of 125 artists, organized by Sigfried Gohr, at the Museum Ludwig

Naples: 'Rooted Rhetoric' exhibition, curated by Gabriele Guercio, with Clegg & Guttmann, Hans Haacke and Joseph Kosuth, at Castel dell' Ovo

1986-87

Pittsburgh: Lothar Baumgarten, *Vacuum*, at the Carnegie Museum of Art

1987

Münster, Germany: 'Skulptur Projekte Münster' exhibition at Westfälisches Landes-museum, organized by Kaspar König and Klaus Bussmann. Includes work by Dennis Adams, Giovanni Anselmo, Michael Asher, Lothar Baumgarten, Luciano Fabro, Ange Leccia, Raimund Kummer and Hermann Pitz

Kassel, Germany: Documenta 8, with an installation by Group Material utilizing works by 47 different artists Paris: 'L'Epoque, La Mode, La Morale, La Passion (1977-87)', exhibition at the Centre Georges Pompidou. Includes work by Dara Birnbaum, Jenny Holzer, Barbara Kruger and Matt Mullican

New York: 'This Is Tomorrow Today' exhibition, at the Clocktower

San Francisco: Jenny Holzer, *The Survival Series* [Moved to London 1988-89]

Essen, Germany: 'Im Auftrag' (By Order) exhibition by Dennis Adams, at the Folkwang Museum

Arnhem, Holland, and Berlin: Barbara Bloom, *Lost and Found*, at the Gemeente Museum, and the DAAD Galerie

Great Britain: 'TSWA 3D' (Television South West Arts) travelling exhibition

1987-90

Los Angeles: Lothar Baumgarten, *Carbon*, at the Museum of Contemporary Art

1988

Holland: 'Sonsbeek 88', site specific projects in the city of Arnhem, Holland

New York: 'The New Urban Landscape' exhibition, at the World Financial Centre. Includes work by Vito Acconci, Dennis Adams, Dan Graham, Joel Otterson and Tadashi Kawamata

Newport Beach, California: 'Chris Burden: A Twenty-Year Survey' exhibition, at the Newport Harbor Art Museum

Los Angeles: Ann Hamilton, *The Capacity of Absorption*

Venice: Venice Biennale, Aperto 88. Includes work by Judith Barry, Barbara Bloom, Mike Kelley and Allan McCollum (225 artists participate)

Paris: 'L'Objet de l'Exposition' exhibition, at the Centre National des Arts Plastiques. Includes work by John Armleder, Bertrand Lavier, Louise Lawler, Ange Leccia, Sherrie Levine

London: 'Edge 88' exhibition, organized by Rob La Frenais. Includes work by Stuart Brisley, Tina Keane, Helen Chadwick, Rose Garrard, Carolee Schneeman, Mona Hatoum and Rasheed Araeen. At Air Gallery

New York: Barbara Bloom, *Seven Deadly Sins*

Kassel, Germany: 'Schlaf der Vernunft' (Sleep of Reason) exhibition, at the Museum Fridericianum. Includes work by Jeff Koons, Haim Steinbach and James Welling

New York: Wolfgang Laib, *The Passageway*

1988-89

Prato, Italy: 'Spazi 88' exhibition, curated by Amnon Barzel. Includes work by Barbara Bloom, Eberhard Bosslet, Klaus vom Bruch, Giorgio Cattani, Philippe Cazal, Carlo Guaita, Kristin Jones and Andrew Ginzel. At the Museo d'Arte Contemporanea Luigi Pecci

1989

Paris: 'Magiciens de la Terre' (Magicians of the Earth) exhibition, curated by Jean-Hubert Martin. At Musée National d'Art Moderne, Centre Georges Pompidou, La Grande Halle, Parc de la Villette

Sao Paulo, Brazil: Sao Paulo Bienale. Includes work by Cildo Meirelles and Tunga

Amsterdam: 'Horn of Plenty: Sixteen Artists from New York City' exhibition, curated by Gosse Oosterhof, at the Stedelijk Museum

Venice: Venice Biennale. Barbara Bloom, *Esprit de l'escalier*

Antwerp, Belgium: 'Beyond the Everyday Object' exhibition, organized by Florent Bex and Rita Compere at the Museum van Hedendaagse Kunst. Includes work by Guillaume Bijl, Pierpaolo Calzolari, Rombouts-Droste, Michel François, Joseph Kosuth, Jannis Kounellis, Ange Leccia, Bruce Nauman, Rainer Ruthenbeck and Jacques Vieille

Los Angeles: 'A Forest of Signs' exhibition, at the Museum of Contemporary Art. Includes work by Dara Birnbaum, Barbara Bloom, Louise Lawler, Sherrie Levine and Matt Mullican

New York: 'Image World: Art and Media Culture' exhibition, at the Whitney Museum of American Art. Includes work by Dennis Adams and others

Nimes, France: James Turrell, *As Above*, *Slant Range*, *First Light*, *Roden Crater*, *The Wait*

1990

Newcastle upon Tyne: 'A New Necessity, First Tyne International Exhibition of Contemporary Art', curated by Declan McGonagle. Includes work by Dennis Adams, Rasheed Araeen, Terry Atkinson, Geneviève Cadieux, Christo, Rose Finn-Kelcey, Dan Graham, Tadashi Kawamata, Matt Mullican and Antoni Muntadas

Chicago: 'Conceptualism - Postconceptualism: The 1960s to the 1990s' exhibition, at the Museum of Contemporary Art

Berlin: 'Die Endlichkeit der Freiheit' (The Finiteness of Freedom) exhibition. Includes work by Giovanni Anselmo, Barbara Bloom, Christian Boltanski, Rebecca Horn, Ilya Kabakov, Mario Merz and Raffael Rheinsberg. First exhibition to open sites in both East and West Berlin after the fall of the wall

Derry, Glasgow, Newcastle upon Tyne, Plymouth: 'Four Cities Project', TSWA exhibition organized by Jonathan Harvey, James Lingwood and Tony Foster. Includes work by Dennis Adams, Judith Barry, Chris Burden, Ron Haselden, Ilya Kabakov, Lee Jaffe, Magdalena Jetelová, Cildo Meirelles and Nancy Spero

London, Glasgow, Newcastle upon Tyne, Rotterdam: 'Edge 90'. Biennial exhibition of projects in the city. Includes work by Marina Abramovic, Guillaume Bijl, Chris Burden, Cornelia Parker, Station House Opera

Montreal: 'The Art of Installation' exhibition, at the Musée d'Art Contemporain

London: 'Seven Obsessions: New Installation Work' exhibition, at the Whitechapel Gallery. Includes work

by Chris Burden, Melanie Counsell, Tim Head and Darrell Viner

Columbus, Ohio: 'New Works for New Spaces: Into the Nineties' exhibition, at the Wexner Centre for the Visual Arts. Includes work by Chris Burden, Ann Hamilton, Sol LeWitt and Christian Marclay

Paris: 'L'Art Conceptuel, Une Perspective' exhibition conceived by Claude Gintz, at the Musée d'Art Moderne de la Ville de Paris

New Orleans: Ann Hamilton, *Linings*
London: Barbara Bloom, *The Reign of Narcissism* (installation), at the Serpentine Gallery

Sydney: 'The Ready-Made Boomerang', 8th Sydney Biennial, at the Art Gallery of New South Wales

London: 'Next Phase' exhibition, curated by Georgie Wise, at Wapping Pumping Station. Includes work by Mark Currah, Anya Gallaccio, Ron Haselden and Gu de Xin

London: 'Modern Medicine' exhibition, at Building One. Includes work by Mat Collishaw, Grainne Cullen, Dominic Denis, Angus Fairhurst, Damien Hirst, Abigail Lane, Miriam Lloyd and Craig Wood

London: Opening of the Museum of Installation

Amsterdam: 'Energies' exhibition, at the Stedelijk Museum. Includes work by Luciano Fabro, Gary Hill and Anselm Kiefer

1991

Pittsburgh: Carnegie International, curated by Lynne Cooke and Mark Francis. Includes work by Lothar Baumgarten, Christian Boltanski, Louise Bourgeois, Sophie Calle, Katharina Fritsch, Ann Hamilton, Allan McCollum, Reinhard Mucha and Maria Nordman. Also includes last major installation by John Cage sited at Mattress Factory

Madrid: 'El Jardin Salvaje' (The Savage Garden) exhibition, curated by Dan Cameron, at the Fundación Caja de Pensiones. Includes work by Judith Barry, Barbara Bloom, Jessica Diamond, Felix Gonzalez-Torres, Ann Hamilton, David Ireland, Mike Kelley, Christian Marclay, Charles Ray and Meg Webster

Berlin: 'Metropolis' exhibition, at Walter Gropius Bau. Includes work by Richard Artschwager, Robert Gober, James Lee Byars, Gary Hill and Jenny Holzer

Christo, *The Umbrellas, Japan-U.S.A., 1984-91*

Charleston, South Carolina: 'Places with a Past' exhibition, at the Spoleto Festival. Includes work by Anthony Gormley, Ann Hamilton and David Hammons

New York: Chris Burden, *The Other Vietnam Memorial*

New York: Sophie Calle, *Ghosts*

New York: Adrian Piper, *What It's Like, What It Is*

New York: Bruce Nauman, *Anthro/Socio*

New York: Ann Hamilton, *Malediction*

Chicago: Judith Barry, *Imagination, Dead Imagine*

New York: Ilya Kabakov, *The Bridge*

New York: Louise Bourgeois, *Twosome*

New York: 'Dislocations', exhibition of installation projects, curated by Robert Storr, at The Museum of Modern Art. Includes work by Louise Bourgeois, Chris Burden, Sophie Calle, David Hammons, Ilya Kabakov, Bruce Nauman and Adrian Piper

1992

London: 'Doubletake: Collective Memory and Current Art' exhibition, at the Hayward Gallery, curated by Lynne Cooke, Bice Curiger and Greg Hilty. Includes works by Sophie Calle, Robert Gober, Ann Hamilton, Gary Hill and Christian Marclay

Madrid and London: 'Edge 92' exhibition. Includes work by Helen Chadwick, Hannah Collins, Fleming & Lapointe and Antoni Muntadas

Kassel, Germany: Documenta 9, curated by Jan Hoet. Includes work by Lothar Baumgarten, Joseph Beuys, Louise Bourgeois, Braco Dimitrijevic, David Hammons, Kazuo Katase, Joseph Kosuth, Mario Merz, Bruce Nauman, Michelangelo Pistoletto and Bill Viola (190 artists from 30 countries)

Los Angeles: 'Helter Skelter: L.A. Art in the 1990s' exhibition, at the Museum of Contemporary Art, organized by Paul Schimmel. Includes work by Chris Burden, Amy Gerstler, Richard Jackson, Mike Kelley, Liz Larner, Paul McCarthy and Nancy Rubins

Zoetermeer, Holland: 'Allocations', at the Floriade World Horticultural Exhibition

New York: 'Fluxus: A Conceptual Country' exhibition, curated by Estera

Milman, at Franklin Furnace Archive

New York: 'Fluxattitudes' exhibition, curated by Cornelia Lauf and Susan Hapgood, at the New Museum of Contemporary Art

London: Ann Hamilton, *Passion*

Washington, D.C.: Ann Hamilton, *Accountings*

Rome: Peter Erskine, *Secrets of the Sun: Millennial Meditations I*

New York: Ilya Kabakov, *Incident at the Museum or Water Music*

1992-93

Washington, D.C.: 'Eva Hesse: A Retrospective, Works 1960-70', at the Hirshhorn Museum

New York: 'The Spatial Drive', exhibition of installations by 11 artists, at The New Museum

Sydney: 'Sydney Biennial: The Boundary Rider', directed by Anthony Bond. Includes work by Giovanni Anselmo, Guillaume Bijl, Border Art Workshop, Helen Chadwick, Wim Delvoye, Anselm Kiefer, Martin Kippenberger, Ken Lum, Adrian Piper, Haim Steinbach, Jan Vercruysse, Rachel Whiteread and Richard Wilson. At the Art Gallery of New South Wales

Chicago: 'Art at the Armory: Occupied Territory' exhibition, organized by Beryl Wright, at the Museum of Contemporary Art. Includes work by Dara Birnbaum, Arnold Crane, Diller & Scofidio, Vernon Fisher, HAHA, Doug Hall, Lynn Hershmann, Gary Hill, Toi Hoang, Jin Soo Kim, Eve Andrée

Laramée, Lazaretto Collaborative, Tatsuo Miyajima, Elizabeth Newman, Michael Shaughnessy, Todt, Francesc Torres and Bill Viola

1993

Holland: 'Sonsbeek '93' exhibition, curated by Valerie Smith. Includes the work of 45 installation artists

New York: 1993 Whitney Biennial. Curated by Elizabeth Sussman. Includes work by Matthew Barney, Chris Burden, Sophie Calle, Robert Gober, Michael Joaquín Grey, Gary Hill, Mike Kelley, Karen Kilimnik, Francesc Torres and Bill Viola. At the Whitney Museum of American Art

Venice: Venice Biennale 1993: Includes work by Louise Bourgeois, James Lee Byars, Hans Haacke, Ilya Kabakov, Allan Kaprow, Yayoi Kusama, Nam June Paik, Jean-Pierre Raynaud and Jan Vercruysse

New York: 'The Great Utopia: The Russian and Soviet Avant Garde, 1915-32' exhibition, at the Solomon R. Guggenheim Museum. Shows constructivist works re-installed in their original configurations

London: 'Gravity and Grace: The Changing Condition of Sculpture 1965-75' exhibition, at the Hayward Gallery. Includes work by Joseph Beuys, Marcel Broodthaers, Jannis Kounellis, Richard Long, Mario Merz, Robert Morris, Reiner Ruthenbeck and Keith Sonnier

New York: Lothar Baumgarten, AMERICA *Invention*, at the Solomon R. Guggenheim Museum

BIBLIOGRAPHY

REFERENCE BOOKS/GENERAL

Apollonio, Umbro, ed. *Futurist Manifestos*. London, 1973

Bachelard, Gaston. *The Poetics of Space*. Boston, 1969; first published in Paris, 1958

Baldauf, Hans, Goodwin, Baker, and Reichert, Amy, eds. *Theatre, Theatricality and Architecture, Perspecta 26*. The Yale Architectural Journal; New York, 1990

Battcock, Gregory, ed. *Minimal Art: A Critical Anthology*. New York, 1968

Battcock, Gregory. *Idea Art: A Critical Anthology*. New York, 1973

Bayer, Herbert, Gropius, Ise, and Gropius, Walter, eds. *Bauhaus 1919-1928*. Boston, 1959

Beardsley, John. *Probing the Earth: Contemporary Land Projects*. Washington, D.C., 1977

—. *Earthworks and Beyond*. New York, 1989

Benjamin, Andrew, ed. *Installation Art*. London, 1993

Berger, Maurice. *Labyrinths: Robert Morris, Minimalism and the 1960s*. New York, 1989

Blazwick, Iwona, ed. *An endless adventure... an endless passion... an endless banquet: A situationist scrapbook*. London, 1989

Buck-Morss, Susan. *The Dialects of Seeing: Walter Benjamin and the Arcades Project*. Cambridge, Mass., 1989

Bürger, Peter. *Theory of the Avant-Garde*. Minneapolis, 1984

Cage, John. *Silence: Lectures and Writings by John Cage*. Cambridge, Mass., and London, 1971

Chip, Herschel B. *Theories of Modern Art*. Berkeley, Los Angeles and London, 1973

Cutts, Simon. *The Unpainted Landscape*. London, 1987

Foster, Hal. *The Anti-Aesthetic: Essays on Postmodern Culture*. Seattle, Wash., 1983

—. *Recodings: Art, Spectacle, Cultural Politics*. Seattle, Wash., 1985

—. *Discussions in Contemporary Culture; No. 1*. Seattle, Wash., and New York, 1987

Goldberg, RoseLee. *Performance: Live Art 1909 to the Present*. London, 1979

Gray, Camilla. *The Russian Experiment in Art*. London, 1971

Groen, F.R., and Munday, R., eds. *Perspecta 23*. New York, 1987

Harrison, Charles, and Wood, Paul, eds. *Art in Theory. 1900-1990: An Anthology of Changing Ideas*. Oxford, 1992

Hendricks, Jon. *Fluxus Codex*. New York, 1989

Henri, Adrian. *Environments and Happenings*. London, 1974

Hertz, Richard. *Theories of Contemporary Art*. Englewood Cliffs, N.J., 1985

Hewison, Robert. *Future Tense: A New Art for the Nineties*.London, 1990

Jameson, Fredric. 'Postmodernism and Utopia', in *Utopia Post-Utopia: Configurations of Nature and Culture in Recent Sculpture and Photography*. Cambridge, Mass., and London, 1988

Kahlen, Wolf. *Ruine der Künste (über Zeit)*. Berlin, 1989

Krauss, Rosalind. *Passages in Modern Sculpture*. Cambridge, Mass., and London, 1981; first published New York, 1977

—. *The Originality of the Avant-Garde and Other Modernist Myths*. Cambridge, Mass., 1986

Kultermann, Udo, trans. John Gabriel. *Art-Events and Happenings*. London, 1971

Leeuw, Reit de, and Beer, Evelyn. *L'Exposition imaginaire: The Art of Exhibiting in the Eighties*. The Hague, 1989

Lippard, Lucy. *Pop Art*. London, 1966

—. *Changing: Essays in Art Criticism*. New York, 1971

—. *Six Years: The Dematerialization of the Art Object from 1966-1972*. New York, 1973

—. *Dwellings*. Philiadelphia, Pa., 1978

McEvilley, Thomas. *Art and Otherness: Crisis in Cultural Identity*. New York, 1992

Meyer, Ursula. *Conceptual Art*. New York, 1972

Michelson, A., *et al.*, eds. *October: The First Decade*. Cambridge, Mass., 1987

Nitsch, Hermann. *Das Orgien Mysterien Theater*. Naples, 1979

O'Doherty, Brian. *Inside the White Cube: The Ideology of the Gallery Space*. Santa Monica and San Francisco, 1976, 1986

Owens, Craig. *Beyond Recognition, Representation, Power and Culture*. Berkeley, Los Angeles and London, 1992

Poggioli, Renato. *The Theory of the Avant-Garde*. Cambridge, Mass., and London, 1968

Rosenberg, Harold. *Artworks and Packages*. Chicago and London, 1969

—. *The De-Definition of Art: Action to Pop to Earthworks*. New York, 1972

—. *Art on the Edge: Creators and Situations*. Chicago and London, 1985

Rosenzweig, Phyllis, and Cooke, Lynne, eds. *Mattress Factory: Installation and Performance 1982-1989*. Pittsburgh, Pa., 1991

Ruhe, Harry. *Fluxus: The Most Radical and Experimental Art Movement of the Sixties*. Amsterdam, 1979

Sayre, Henry M. *The Object of Performance: The American Avant-Garde Since 1970*. Chicago and London, 1989

Sonfist, Alan, ed. *Art on the Land: A Critical Anthology of Environmental Art*. New York, 1983

Sowers, Robert. *Rethinking the Forms of Visual Expression*. Berkeley, Calif., 1990

Stearns, Robert, dir.; Howell, John, guest ed. *Breakthroughs: Avant-Garde Artists in Europe and America 1950-1990*. Ohio and New York, 1991

Vergo, Peter, ed. *The New Museology*. London, 1989

Wallis, Brian, ed. *Art after Modernism: Rethinking Representation*. New York and Boston, 1984

—. *Blasted Allegories: An Anthology of Writings by Contemporary Artists*. New York and Cambridge, Mass., 1987

Williams, Emmett. *My Life in Flux - and Vice Versa*. London, 1992

Wines, James. *De-Architecture*. New York, 1987

BOOKS BY ARTISTS

Acconci, Vito. *Leap/Think/Rethink/Fall*.Dayton, Ohio, 1979

Anselmo, Giovanni. *116 Particolari Visibili e Misurabili di Infinito*. Turin, 1975

Antin, Eleanor. *Being Antinova*. Los Angeles, 1983

— *The Antinova Plays*. Los Angeles, 1987

Asher, Michael. *Writings 1973-1983 on Works 1969-1979*. Ed. Benjamin Buchloh. Halifax, Nova Scotia, 1983

Baumgarten, Lothar. AMERICA *Invention*. New York, 1993

Bloom, Barbara. *The Reign of Narcissism*. Stuttgart and London, 1990

—. *Never Odd or Even*. Ed. Daniela Goldmann. Munich and The Carnegie Museum of Art, Pittsburgh, Pa., 1992

Boltanski, Christian. *Les Morts pour rire*. Antibes, 1975

—. *20 Règles et techniques*. Copenhagen, 1975

Broodthaers: Writings, Interviews, Photographs. Ed. Benjamin Buchloh. Cambridge, Mass., and London, 1988

Burden, Chris. *Chris Burden 71-73*. Los Angeles, 1974

—. *Chris Burden 74-77*. Los Angeles, 1978

Buren, Daniel. *Daniel Buren: Legend, Vol. I and II*. London, 1973

—. *Daniel Buren: Voile/Toile, Toile/Voile*. With Bernd Mahr and Horst Merten. Berlin, 1975

—. *Daniel Buren*. Ed. Pagé, Suzanne. 42e Venice Biennale, Association Française d'Action Artistique, 1986

Christo, Packed Tower, Sporeto. New York, 1970

Christo. *Christo*. With text by David Bourdon. New York, 1970

—. *Christo: Valley Curtain*. New York, 1973

—. *Ocean Front*. With text by Sally Yard and Sam Hunter. Princeton, N.J., 1975

Christo: Running Fence. With text by Calvin Tomkins and David Bourdon. New York, 1978

Christo: Wrapped Walk Ways. New York, 1978

Christo, Surrounded Islands, Biscayne Bay, Greater Miami, Florida, 1980-83. With an essay by Jonathan Fineberg. New York, 1986

D'Agostino, Peter, and Muntadas, Antoni. *The Un/Necessary Image*. New York, 1982

Dimitrijevic, Braco. *An Obelisk Beyond History*. West Berlin, 1979

Duchamp, Marcel. *Etant Donnés*. Philadelphia Museum of Art, 1987

Fabro, Luciano. *Regole d'Arte*. Milan, 1980

David Goldenberg: Microwave & Freezerstills. Ed. Museum of Installation. London, 1992

Graham, Dan. *Selected Works: 1965-72*. New York, 1972

—. *Rock My Religion*. Cambridge, Mass., 1993

Haacke, Hans. *Framing and Being Framed: 7 Works 1970-75*. Halifax, Nova Scotia, and New York, 1975

—. *Hans Haacke: 4 Works 1978-79*. New York, 1979

Damien Hirst. Institute of Contemporary Arts/Jay Jopling, London, 1991

Holzer, Jenny. *A Little Knowledge*. New York, 1979

—. *Truisms and Essays*. Halifax, Nova Scotia, 1983

Vault: Chris Jennings. Ed. Museum of Installation. London, 1991

Judd, Donald. *Complete Writings 1959-1975*. Halifax, Nova Scotia, and New York,1975

Kosuth, Joseph. *Art after Philosophy and After: Collected Writings, 1966-1990*. Cambridge, Mass., and London, 1991

Jannis Kounellis. With text by R.H.Fuchs. Amsterdam, 1981

Kruger, Barbara. *Picture/ Readings*. New York, 1978

—. *No Progress in Pleasure*. New York, 1982

—. *Beauty and Critique*. New York, 1983

Leccia, Ange. *Arrangement*. Houston, 1992

LeWitt, Sol. *Arcs, Circles and Grids*. Berne, 1972

Long, Richard. *Richard Long in Conversation*. Bristol and Noordvoijk, 1985

—. *Lines of Time*. Amsterdam, 1986

—. *Stone Water Miles*. Geneva, 1987

Marclay, Christian. *Footsteps*. Zurich, 1989

Merz, Mario. *La Frutta e qui...*. Ed. Lucio Amelio. Naples, 1976

Nauman, Bruce. *Pictures of Sculptures in a Room*. Davis, Calif., 1966

—. *Clear Sky*. San Francisco, 1968

—. *L.A. Air*. Los Angeles, 1970

Paik, Nam June. *An Anthology of Nam June Paik*. With an essay by Hohn G. Hanhardt. Tokyo, 1984

Penone, Giuseppe. *Rovesciare gli occhi*. With Jean-Christophe Ammanno. Turin, 1977

Perejaume. *Perejaume*. Galeria Joan Prats, Barcelona, 1990

Simonds, Charles. *3 Peoples*. Genoa, 1955

—. *Art/Cahier 2: Charles Simonds*. Paris, 1975

The Writings of Robert Smithson. Ed. Nancy Holt. New York, 1979

Sonnier, Keith. *Object-Situation-Object 1969-70*. Cologne, 1972

Thek, Paul. *A Document Made by Paul Thek and Edwin Klein*. Amsterdam and Stockholm, 1969

Tremlett, David. *Restless*. London, 1983

—. *The Mjimwema Drawings*. Ghent, 1991

—. *Abandoned Drawings*. Amiens, 1993

Tschumi, Bernard, and Goldberg, RoseLee. *A Space: A Thousand Words*. Italy, 1975

Vostell, Wolf. *Aktionen, Happenings und Demonstrationen seit 1965*. Reinbeck, West Germany, 1970

Wodiczko, Krzysztof. *Homeless Vehicle Project, Homeless Conversations*. With Rudolph Luria. New York, 1988

MONOGRAPHS

Adriani, G., Konnertz, W., and Thomas, K., eds. *Joseph Beuys: Life and Works*. New York, 1973

Ahrens, Carsten, and Haenlein, Carl, eds. *Klaus vom Bruch*. Hanover, 1990

Armstrong, Richard. *Artschwager, Richard*. Whitney Museum of American Art, New York, 1988

Beeren, Wim. *Walter de Maria*. Museum Boysmans-van Beuningen, Rotterdam, 1984

Berger, Maurice. *Labyrinths: Robert Morris, Minimalism and the 1960s*. New York, 1989

Blazwick, Iwona, ed. *Public Fantasy: An Anthology of Critical Essays, Fictions and Project Descriptions by Judith Barry*. London, 1991

Blistene, Bernard. *Fontana*. Musée Nationale d'Art Moderne, Centre Georges Pompidou, Paris, 1988

Brown, Julia, ed. *Occluded Front: James Turrell*. Los Angeles, 1985

Byars, James Lee. Michael Werner Gallery, Cologne, 1985

Celant, Germano. *Claes Oldenburg: A Bottle of Notes and Some Voyages*. New York, 1988

—. *Pistoletto*. New York, 1988

—. *Mario Merz*. New York and Milan, 1989

Cohen, Françoise, Lapalus, Marie, and Miloux, Yannick, eds. *Bill Culbert*. Musée des Beaux-Arts André Malraux, Le Havre, 1990

Compton, M. *Yves Klein 1928-1962: Selected Writings*. Tate Gallery, London, 1974

Dieterich, Barbara, *et al.*, eds. *Vostell Retrospektive 1958-1974*. Neuer Berliner Kunstverein, Berlin, 1974

Elderfield, John. *Kurt Schwitters*. London, 1987

Elliot, James. *The Perfect Thought: Works by James Lee Byars*. University Art Museum, University of California, Berkeley, 1990

Fabro, Luciano. *Fabro: Works 1963-1986*. Fruitmarket Gallery, Edinburgh; Umberto Allemandi Co., Turin, 1986

Felix, Z., and Oxenaar, R.W.D., eds. *Michael Heizer*. Museum Folkwang, Essen; Rijksmuseum Kröller-Müller, Otterlo, Netherlands, 1979

Fuchs, Rudi H. *Ulrich Rückriem: Skulpturen 1968-78*. Essen, 1978

Goldwater, Marge. *Marcel Broodthaers*. New York, 1989

Gough-Cooper, Jennifer, and Caumont, Jacques. *Ephemerides on and about Marcel Duchamp and Rrose Sélavy 1887-1986*. Hulton, Pontus, curator. *Marcel Duchamp*. Milan and London, 1993

Guillot, Jacques. *Jean-Luc Vilmouth: Local Time*. Centre National D'Art Contemporain de Grenoble, 1987

Gumpert, Lynn. *Christian Boltanski: Reconstitution*. Whitechapel Gallery, London; von Abbemuseum, Eindhoven; Musée de Grenoble, 1990

Hanhardt, John G. *Francesc Torres: The Head of the Dragon (Anthology)*. Museo Nacional Centro de Arte Reina Sofia, Madrid, 1991

Hovdenakk, Per. *Per Barclay: Installations with Motor Oil*. Hoevikodden, Norway, 1991

Hulton, Pontus, curator. *Marcel Duchamp*. Milan and London, 1993. Gough-Cooper, Jennifer, and Caumont, Jacques. *Ephemerides on and about Marcel Duchamp and Rrose Sélavy 1887-1986*

Tadashi Kawamata: Projects 1982-1990. Annely Juda Fine Art, London, 1990

König, Kasper. *Yvonne Rainer: Work 1961-73*. Halifax, Nova Scotia, and New York, 1974

Krauss, Rosalind. *Eva Hesse, 1936-1970: Sculptures and Drawings*. Kestner Gesellschaft, Hanover, 1979

Kuspit, Donald B. *Fischl*. New York, 1987

Mirotchnikoff, F., Parsy, P.H., and Vilmouth, J.L., eds. *Jean-Luc Vilmouth*. Musée Nationale d'Art Moderne, Centre Georges Pompidou, Paris, 1992

Mock, Jean-Yves. *Yves Klein*. Musée Nationale d'Art Moderne, Centre Georges Pompidou, Paris, 1983

Bruce Nauman: Werke von 1965 bis 1986. With essays by Jean-Christophe Ammann, Nicholas Serota and Joan Simon. Basle, 1986

Nusser, Uta, ed. *Wolfgang Laib*. Stuttgart, 1989

Passuth, Krisztina. *Moholy-Nagy*. London and New York,1987

Patteeuw, Roland, ed. *Marie-Jo Lafontaine: Videosculptures*. Stichting Kunst en Projecten, Belgium, 1987

Pontbraind, Chantal. *Geneviève Cadieux: Canada XLIV Biennale Di Venezia*. Musée des Beaux-Arts de Montréal, Montreal, 1990

Risso, B. *Lucio Fabro*. Turin,1980

Rose, Barbara. *Claes Oldenburg*. Museum of Modern Art, New York, 1970

Tisdale, Caroline. *Joseph Beuys*. London, 1979

van Mulders, Wim, ed. *Guillaume Bijl*. Galerie Isy Brachot, Brussels, 1989

Wheldon, Keith, and Petry, Michael. *Objective Installations*. Museum of Installation, London, 1990

Wolf Vostell: environment, video, peintures, dessins 1977-85. With texts by Michael Marschall, Nadine Lehni and Michel Giroud. Strasbourg, 1986

EXHIBITION CATALOGUES

Allthorpe-Guyton, Marjorie. *Edge 88*. Performance Magazine, London, 1988

Armstrong, R., *et al.*, eds. *1989 Biennial Exhibition*. Whitney Museum of American Art, New York, 1989

Barron, Stephanie, and Tuchman, Maurice, eds. *The Museum as Site: Sixteen Projects*. Los Angeles County Museum, Los Angeles, 1981

Barzel, Amnon, curator. *Spaces '88*. Museo d'Arta Contemporanea, Prato, Centro/Electra, 1988

Basaglia, Enrico, and Keller, Giovanni, eds. *Arte e Scienza*. Venice Biennale; Venice, 1986

Bex, Florent, and Friedel, Helmut. *Naakte Schoonheid/ Paradoxe des Alltags*. Museum van Hedendaagse Kunst, Ghent; Städtische Galerie im Lenbachhaus, Munich, 1991

Bex, Florent. *Beyond the Everyday Object*. Museum van Hedendaagse Kunst, Ghent, 1989

Billeter, Erika. *Mythos und Ritual in der Kunst der 70er Jahre*. Kunsthaus, Zurich, 1981.

Bonito Oliva, Achille, curator. *Punti Cardinali dell'Arte*. Venice Biennale; Venice, 1993

Brett, Guy. *Transcontinental: An Investigation of Reality. Nine Latin American Artists*. London and New York, 1990

Bronson, A.A., and Gale, Peggy, eds. *Museums by Artists*. Art Gallery of Ontario, Toronto, 1983

Brown, Carol, and Summerbell, Deirdre, eds. *Un-Natural Traces: Contemporary Art from Canada*. Barbican Art Gallery, London, 1991

Brüderlin, Markus, Loers, Veit, and Burckhardt, Lucius. *Der Schlaf der Vernunft*. Museum Fridericianum, Kassel, Germany, 1989

Bussmann, Klaus, and König, Kasper. *Skulpturprojekte in Münster*. Cologne, 1987

Cameron, Dan. *Horn of Plenty: Sixteen Artists from New York City*. Stedelijk Museum, Amsterdam, 1989

—. *NY Art Now*. Saatchi Collection, London, 1988

—. *El Jardin Salvaje (The Savage Garden)*. Fundación Caja Pensiones, Madrid, 1990

Cameron, Stuart, Coppock, Christopher, and Spencer Davis, Jenni, eds. *Radical Chip: Contemporary Art From Japan*. Chapter Gallery, Ffotogallery, Oriel, Caerdydd, Wales, 1991

Celant, Germano. *Dal Futurismo alla Body Art*. Venice Biennale; Venice, 1977

—. *Unexpressionism: Art Beyond the Contemporary*. New York, 1988

Celant, Germano, Linker, Kate, and Owens, Craig. *Implosion: A Postmodern Perspective*. Moderna Museet, Stockholm, 1987

Chambers, Eddie. *Four x 4: Installations by Sixteen Artists in Four Galleries*. Arnolfini Gallery, Bristol, 1992

Clot, Manel. *Timespan: Jenny Holzer, On Kawara, Bruce Nauman, Lawrence Weiner*. Fundacio Caixa de Pensions, Barcelona, 1990

Compton, Michael. *New Art at the Tate*. London, 1983

Cooke, Lynne, and Francis, Mark, eds. *Carnegie International 1991*. New York, 1991

Cooke, Lynne, Curiger, Bice, and Hilty, Greg, eds. *Doubletake: Collective Memory and Current Art*. South Bank Centre, London, 1992

The Coracle. Coracle Press Gallery, 1973-1987. Coracle, London, and Yale Centre for British Art, New Haven, 1989

Davis, Hugh, Onorato, Ronald, and Yard, Sally, eds. *Sitings*. La Jolla Museum of Contemporary Art, Los Angeles, 1986

de Zegher, Cathy, ed. *Tunga: lezarts/Cildo Meireles* Kanaal Art Foundation, Kortrijk, Belgium, 1989

Enneper, Mic. *Lager 50°56' / 6°57' NORD-OST*. Josef-Haubrich-Kunsthalle Köln, Cologne, 1991

Fox, Howard. *A Primal Spirit: Ten Contemporary Japanese Sculptors*. Los Angeles County Museum of Art, 1990

Francis, Mark, and Newman, Michael. *The Mirror and the Lamp*. The Fruitmarket Gallery, Edinburgh/Lecturis, 1986

Fuchs, Rudi, and Bos, Saskia, eds. *Documenta 7*. Kassel, West Germany, 1982

Garrels, Gary. *Beyond the Monument*. Cambridge, Mass., 1983

—. *New Sculpture*. The Renaissance Society at the University of Chicago, 1986

Gintz, Claude, Laffon, Juliette, and Scherf, Angeline, eds. *L'Art Conceptuel: une perspective*. Musée d'Art de la Ville de Paris, 1990

Green, Renée. *World Tour*. Museum of Contemporary Art, Los Angeles, 1993

Gudis, Catherine, ed.; Goldstein, Ann, and Jacob, Mary Jane, curators. *A Forest of Signs: Art in the Crisis of Representation*. Cambridge, Mass., and London, 1989

Gudis, Catherine, ed. *Helter Skelter, LA Art in the 1990s*. Museum of Contemporary Arts, Los Angeles, 1992

Hall, Douglas. *Edinburgh International: Reason and Emotion in Contemporary Art*. Royal Scottish Academy, Edinburgh, 1988

Heimat. Wewerka & Weiss Galerie, Berlin, 1991

Heiss, Alanna. *Casino Fantasma*. Institute of Contemporary Arts, New York, 1990

Hoet, Jan. *Chambres d'Amis*. Museum van Hedendaagse Kunst, Ghent, Belgium, 1986

Horky, Dieter. *Köln-Kunst 88*. Cologne, 1988

Kardon, Janet, *et al. Urban Encounters: Art, Architecture, Audience*. Philadelphia Institute of Contemporary Art/University of Pennsylvania, 1980

König, Kasper. *Westkunst: Art Since 1939*, Vol. II (Heute), Wallraf-Richartz Museum, Cologne, 1981

Lawler, Louise, and McCollum, Allan. *For Presentation and Display: Ideal Settings*. Diane Brown Gallery, New York, 1984

Licht, Jennifer. *Spaces*. Museum of Modern Art, New York, 1969

Lingwood, James. *TSWA Four Cities Project: New Work for Different Places*. TSWA Ltd, Newcastle upon Tyne, 1990

McGonagle, Declan, dir. *First Tyne International: A New Necessity*. Newcastle upon Tyne, 1990

Martin, Richard, ed. *The New Urban Landscape, The World Financial Centre*. Battery Park, New York, 1988

Martin, Jean-Hubert, Francis, Mark, and McEvilley, Thomas. *Magiciens de la Terre*. Centre Georges Pompidou, Paris, 1989

Metgen, Günter. *Documenta 8: Exhibition Guide*. Kassel, West Germany, 1987

Monte, James, and Tucker, Marcia, eds. *Anti-Illusion: Procedures - Materials*. Whitney Museum of American Art, New York, 1969

Nachtigäller, Roland, and von Velsen, Nicola, eds. *Documenta 9*. Stuttgart and New York, 1992

Nairne, Sandy. *State of the Art: Ideas & Images in the 1980s*. London, 1987

The New Sculpture 1965-1975. Whitney Museum of American Art, New York, 1990

Ochsler, Monika. *The Archaeology of Silence: Multi-Media Installations of Contemporary Art*. London, 1991

Parmesani, Loredana, ed. *Arte Italiana 1960-1982*. London, 1982

Rasponi, Simonetta, ed. *Dimensione Futuro, L'Artista e lo Spazzio*. Venice Biennale; Venice, 1990

Reinhardt, Debra. *Ten Sites: Works, Artists, Years*. Laumeier Sculpture Park, St Louis, Mo., 1992

Ross, David A. *Between Spring and Summer: Soviet Conceptual Art in the Era of Late Communism*. Tacoma Art Museum; Cambridge, Mass., and London, 1990

Ryan, Marianne, ed. *Gravity and Grace: The Changing Condition of Sculpture 1965-1975*. South Bank Centre/Arts Council of Great Britain, London, 1993

Sartorius, Joachim, and Tannert, Christoph, eds. *Die Endlichkeit der Freiheit: Berlin 1990. Ein Austellungsprojekt in Ost und West*. Berlin, 1990

Storr, Robert. *Dislocations*. Museum of Modern Art, New York, 1991

Tupitsyn, Margarita. *The Work of Art in the Age of Perestroika*. Phyllis Kind Gallery, New York, 1990

Utopia Post-Utopia: Configurations of Nature and Culture in Recent Sculpture and Photography. Cambridge, Mass., and London, 1988

Walser, Rupert, ed. *Reclining Red: Non Objective Painting and Sculpture*. Goethe Institute, London, 1989

Wise, Georgie. *Next Phase*. E.G.A., London, 1990

Wontz, Melinda. *Architectural Sculpture: Projects*. Los Angeles Institute of Contemporary Art, 1980

EXHIBITION CATALOGUES (ONE PERSON SHOW)

Vito Acconci. Stedelijk Museum, Amsterdam, 1978

—. *Vito Acconci: Domestic Trappings*. With an essay by R.J. Onorato. La Jolla, California, 1987

Adelman, Irene. *Kazuo Katase*. Centre National D'Art Contemporain, Grenoble, 1989

Avgikos, Jan. *Joseph Kosuth: Three Installations: 1970, 1979 and 1988*. Rubin Spangle Gallery, New York, 1991

Ayot, Pierre. Musée d'Art Contemporain, Montreal, 1980

Barents, Els. *Lothar Baumgarten: Tierra de los perros mudos*. Stedelijk Museum, Amsterdam, 1985

Block, René. *Jaroslaw Kozlowski: The Show The Exhibition*. DAAD Galerie, Berlin, 1985

Christian Boltanski: Leçon des Ténèbres. Munich, 1986

Bonaventura, P., Jaar, A., and Lampert, C., eds. *Alfredo Jaar: Two or Three Things I Imagine About Them*. Whitechapel Art Gallery, London, 1992

Brock, Bazon. *Mondo Cane: Neun Bilder von Gerhard Merz*. Galerie Tanit, Munich, 1983

Bronson, A., Partz, F., and Zontal, J. *General Idea: The Public and Private Domains of the Miss General Idea Pavilion*. Artspace, San Francisco, California, 1988

Marcel Broodthaers. With complete bibliography. Cologne, 1980

Buren, Daniel. *Sketches for a Work in Situ*. Serpentine Gallery, London, 1987

Sophie Calle. With essays by Hervé Guibert and Yve-Alain Bois. Musée d'art Moderne de la Ville de Paris (A.R.C.), 1991

Cameron, Dan. *The Savage Garden* (Christian Marclay). Fundación Caja de Pensiones, Madrid, 1991

Celant, Germano. *Piero Manzoni: Paintings, Reliefs and Objects*. Tate Gallery, London, 1974

Compton, Michael. *Marcel Broodthaers*. Tate Gallery, London, 1980

Tony Cragg. With Lynne Cooke. London, 1987

de Domizio Durini, Lucrezia. *Olivestone: Joseph Beuys*. Rome, 1992

D'Harnoncourt, Anne, and Hopps, Walter. *Reflections on a New Work by Marcel Duchamp*. Philadelphia Museum of Art, Bulletin Vol. LXIV Nos. 299 and 300, 1987

de Loisy, Jean. *Ian Hamilton Finlay. Revolutionary Poursuits*. Fondation Cartier pour l'Art Contemporain, Paris, 1987

Walter de Maria: The 5-7-9 Series. Gagosian Gallery, New York, 1992

de Oliveira, Nicolas, Oxley, Nicola, and Petry, Michael, eds. *Max Couper: The Endless Conveyor*. Museum of Installation, London, 1991

Braco Dimitrijevic. With text by David Brown. London, 1985

Douroux, Xavier. *Imi Knoebel: Eigentum Himmelreich*. Le consortium / Musée municipale, La Roche-sur-Yon, 1984

Fabre, Jan. Galerie Ronny van de Velde & Co., Antwerp, 1988

Homage to Ian Hamilton-Finlay. With essay by Yves Abrioux. London, 1987

Fisher, Jean. *Tina Keane: Escalator*. Riverside Studios, London, 1988

Flood, Richard. *Robert Gober*. Serpentine Gallery, London; Tate Gallery, Liverpool, 1993

Ford, Jacqueline. *Edward Allington: In Pursuit of Savage Luxury*. Nottingham, 1984

General Idea 1968-1984. Basle, 1984

Robert Gober. Museum Boymans-van Beuningen, Rotterdam; Kunsthalle, Berne, 1990

Haacke, Hans. 'Museum, Managers of Consciousness', in *Hans Haacke: Unfinished Business*. Ed. Brian Wallis. New York, 1986

Harris, Susan. *Dennis Adams: The Architecture of Amnesia*. Kent Fine Art Inc., New York, 1990

Haselden, Ron. *Thames Project*. Foundation De Appel, Amsterdam, 1981

Haskell, Barbara. *James Turrell: Light and Space*. Whitney Museum of American Art, New York, 1981

Head, Tim. *The Tyranny of Reason*. Institute of Contemporary Arts, London, 1985

Helfenstein, Josef, and Schenker, Christoph. *James Turrell: First Light*. Berne, 1991

Hill, Gary. *And Sat Down Beside Her*. Galerie des Archives, Paris, 1990

Himmel, Eric, ed. *Christo, The Pont Neuf, Wrapped*. Cologne, 1990

Jenny Holzer: The Venice Installation. With an essay by Michael Anpling and text by the artist. Albright-Knox Art Gallery, Buffalo, N.Y., 1990

Hopper, Robert, dir. *Magdalena Jetelová*. The Henry Moore Sculpture Trust, Halifax, U.K., 1991

Rebecca Horn: La Ferdinanda: Sonate für eine Medici-Villa. With texts by Katharine Schmidt and Germano Celant. Baden-Baden, West Germany, 1981

Jehle, Werner. *Guillaume Bijl: Installation*. Galerie Klaus Littmann, Basel, Switzerland, 1990

Anish Kapoor: Recent Sculpture and Drawings. With an essay by Helaine Posner. Amherst, Mass., 1986

Kotik, Charlotta. *Louise Bourgeois*. Venice Biennale; The Brooklyn Museum, New York, 1993

Jannis Kounellis. With texts by Zdenek Felix and Bruno Cora. Essen, West Germany, 1979

Eve Laramée: Venusian Lagoons. The Albuquerque Museum, New Mexico, 1983

Leclerc, Fabienne, ed. *Richard Venlet*. Galerie des Archives, Paris, 1990

Sol LeWitt 1968-84. Amsterdam, 1984

Lingwood, James. *Ilya Kabakov: 10 Characters*. Institute of Contemporary Arts, London, 1989

McEvilley, Thomas, and Allthorpe-Guyton, Marjorie. *Anish Kapoor*. XLIV Venice Biennale; The British Council, London, 1990

Loren Madsen: Sculptures/Installations. David McKee Gallery, New York, 1986

Mari, Bartomeu, and Brayer, Marie-Ange. *Judith Barry: The Work of the Forest*. Fondation pour l'Architecture à Bruxelles, Belgium, 1992

Martin, Jean-Hubert. *Dan Graham: Pavilions*. Kunsthalle, Berne, 1983

Gordon Matta-Clark. IVAM, Centre Julio Gonzalez, Valencia, Spain, 1993

Merz, Mario. *Tables from Drawings of Mario Merz*. John Weber Gallery, New York; Jack Wendler Gallery, London, 1973

Mario Merz. With an interview by Jean-Christoph Ammann and Suzanne Pagé. Paris, 1981

Meschede, Friederich. *Peter Zimmermann: Bilder und Objekte*. Westfälischer Kunstverein, Münster, 1992

Newman, Michael. *Richard Wilson*. Matt's Gallery, London, 1989

Obussier, Claire, and Watkins, Jonathan. *Vong Phaophanit: What Falls to the Ground but can't be eaten*. Chisenhale Gallery, London, 1991

Onwin, Glen. *As Above, So Below*. The Henry Moore Sculpture Trust, Halifax, U.K., 1991

Overy, Paul, Roberts, John, and Hood, Stuart. *Stuart Brisley*. Institute of Contemporary Arts, London, 1981

Parker, Cornelia. *Cold Dark Matter: An Exploded View*. Chisenhale Gallery, London, 1991

Renton, Andrew, and Petry, Michael. *Michael Petry: The Chemistry of Love*. The James Hockey Gallery, WSCAD, Farnham, 1992

Safran, Yehuda, ed. *Frederick Kiesler 1890-1965*. Architectural Association, London, 1989

Schneede, Uwe M., and Bertuleit, Sigrid, eds. *Raimund Kummer*. Hamburger Kunsthalle, 1991

Charles Simonds. With essays by John Hallmark-Neff, Daniel Abadie and John Beardsley. Chicago, 1982

Stooss, Toni. *Rebecca Horn*. Kunsthaus Zurich, 1983

James Turrell. With an essay by Claude Gintz. Paris, 1983

James Turrell: Mapping Spaces/Kartographie des Raumes. With texts by Craig Adcock, Jean-Christophe Ammann and others. New York and Basle, 1987

Counter-Monuments: Krzysztof Wodiczko's Public Projections. Cambridge, Mass., 1987

MAGAZINE ARTICLES

Als, Hilton. 'Darling' (Adrian Piper), in *Artforum* (March 1991): 100-104

Archer, Michael. 'The Divided Meadows of Aphrodite' (Ian Hamilton-Finlay), in *Artforum* (November 1991): 90-95

—. 'Christian Marclay', in *Art Monthly* (April 1991): 19

Avgikos, Jan. 'The New Sculpture 1965-75 - Did It Live up to Its Own Expectations?', in *Flash Art* (Summer 1990): 138-39

Berger, Maurice. 'The Critique of Pure Racism. An Interview with Adrian

Piper', in *Afterimage* (October 1990): 5-9

Bernard, David. 'HaHa: The Rest is Silence' in *Flash Art* (November/December 1991): 125

Blase, Christoph. 'Gerhard Merz at the Kunstverein (Munich)', in *Artscribe* (January/February 1987): 81

Bonami, Francesco. 'Matthew Barney - The Artist as a Young Athlete', in *Flash Art* (January/February 1992): 100-103

—. 'Angela Bullock - Lonesome Comedy', in *Flash Art* (March/April 1992): 96-97

—. 'Who Is Jessica Diamond and Why Is She Saying Those Terrible Things about Us?', in *Flash Art* (January/February 1993): 62-63

—. 'Robert Irwin, Justin Ladda, Robert Gober, Ilya Kabakov - Pop Art', in *Flash Art* (January/February 1993): 86-87

Borden, Lizzie. 'A Note on David Tremlett's Work', in *Studio International* (June 1983): 289-91

Bourgeois, Louise. 'Freud's Toys', in *Artforum* (January 1990): 111-113

Bourriaud, Nicolas. 'Karen Kilimnik - Psycho-Splatter', in *Flash Art* (March/April 1992): 88-90

Buchloh, Benjamin H.D. 'Beuys: The Twilight of the Idol', in *Artforum* (January 1980): 39-40

Buren, Daniel. 'The Function of the Studio', in *October* 10 (Fall 1979)

Cameron, Dan. 'Mike Kelley's Art of Violation', in *Arts Magazine* (June 1986): 14-17

—. 'Through the Looking Glass, Darkly: Fischli/Weiss', in *Artforum* (September 1992): 67-69

—. 'The Hassle in Kassel - Documenta IX', in *Artforum* (September 1992): 86-89

—. 'David Hammons, Coming in from the Cold', in *Flash Art* (January/February 1993): 68-71

Cary, Katrina F.C. 'Ilya Kabakov: Profile of a Soviet Unofficial Artist', in *Art & Auction* (February 1987): 86-87

Celant, Germano. 'The Inside Skinside' (Wim Delvoye), in *Artforum* (Summer 1991): 87-90

Cembalest, Robin. 'The Man Who Flew into Space', in *Artnews* (May 1990): 176-81

Crockett, Tobey. 'The Dark Side of Dennis Oppenheim', in *Artforum* (December 1991): 68-73

Dannat, Adrian. 'Wim Delvoye - A Tile of Shit', in *Flash Art* (Summer 1992): 80-83

Deitcher, David. 'Barbara Kruger: Resisting Arrest', in *Artforum* (February 1991): 84-91

—. 'Art on the Installation Plan', in *Artforum* (January 1992): 78-84

de Maria, Walter. 'The Lightning Field: Some Facts, Notes, Data, Information, Statistics and Statements', in *Artforum* (April 1980): 58

Drucker, Johanna. 'Spectacle and Subjectivity - The Work of Judith Barry', in *Artscribe* (March/April 1991): 41-43

Fischl, Eric. 'The Man Who Exposes Himself to Women', in *Normal* (Summer 1987)

Francblin, Catherine. 'Raynaud's Psycho-Objects', in *Art in America* (June 1991): 114-21

Gardner, Colin. 'The Space Between Words: Lawrence Weiner', in

Artforum (November 1990): 156-60

Goldberg, RoseLee. 'Space as Praxis', in *Studio International* 190, no. 977 (September/October 1975): 130-35

Grimes, Nancy. 'A Walk through Borofsky's Brain', in *Artnews* (Summer 1985)

Gumpert, Lynn. 'Accidental History' (Braco Dimitrijevic), in *Art in America* (June 1991): 122-29

Howell, John. 'Mike Kelley, Plato's Cave, Rothko's Chapel, Lincoln's Profile', in *Artforum* (May 1987): 151-52

Johnson, Ken. 'Generational Saga' (Whitney Biennial), in *Art in America* (June 1991): 44-51

Jones, Kellie. 'David Hammons', in *Real Life Magazine* (Autumn 1986): 2-9

Kirili, Alain. 'The Passion for Sculpture - A Conversation with Louise Bourgeois', in *Arts* (March 1989): 68-75

Kontova, Helen, and Politi, Giancarlo. 'Allan Kaprow - Happens to be an Artist', in *Flash Art* (January/February 1992): 92-95

Kuspik, Donald. 'The Modern Fetish' (Haim Steinbach), in *Artforum* (October 1988): 132-40

Lewis, James. 'Beyond Redemption' (Mike Kelley), in *Artforum* (Summer 1991): 71-75

Lieberman, Rhonda. 'The Loser Thing' (Cary S. Leibowitz/ Candyass), in *Artforum* (September 1992): 86-89

Liebmann, Lisa. 'Grand Elisions' (Keith Sonnier), in *Artforum* (April 1992): 88-91

Lippard, Lucy R. 'Louise Bourgeois:

From the Inside Out', in *Artforum* (March 1975): 26-33

Lloyd, Jill. 'An Interview with Ilya Kabakov: The "Untalented Artist" - A Schizophrenic Way of Life', in *Art International* (Autumn 1989): 70-73

Marmer, Nancy. 'The Art of Deception' (James Turrell), in *Art in America* (May 1981)

Miller, John. 'What You Don't See Is What You Get: Allan McCollum's Surrogates, Perpetual Photos and Perfect Vehicles', in *Artscribe* (January/February 1987): 32-36

Mitchell, W.J.T. 'The Pictorial Turn', in *Artforum* (March 1992): 89-94

Nickas, Robert. 'R.I.P. (Rest in Pieces) Some Scattered Thoughts on the End of Scatter Art', in *Flash Art* (Summer 1992): 84-85

Nittve, Lars. 'All Fives, Sevens and Nines' (Walter de Maria), in *Artforum* (Summer 1992): 70-73

Pincus-Witten, Robert. 'Bruce Nauman: Another Kind of Reasoning', in *Artforum* (February 1971): 30-37

Plagens, Peter. 'Michael Asher: The Thing of It Is...', in *Artforum* (April 1972)

—. 'Keith Sonnier: Video and Film as Colourfield', in *Artforum* (May 1972)

Renton, Andrew. 'Tatsuo Miyajima - Counter Culture', in *Flash Art* (March/April 1992): 106

Sayer, Henry. 'Antinova Dances Again', in *Artweek*, 31 May 1986

Schenker, Christophe. 'Guillaume Bijl: Object of Desire', in *Flash Art* (January/February 1991): 128

—. 'Imi Knoebl: The Limits of Communicability', in *Flash Art*

(November/December 1991): 103-107

Schorr, Collier. 'Lockdown - Robert Gober at Dia', in *Artforum* (February 1993): 89-93

Schwartzman, Allan. 'Ann Hamilton, Room for Interpretation', in *Interview* (December 1991): 42

Sharp, Willoughby. 'Structure and Sensibility: An Interview with Jannis Kounellis', in *Avalanche* (Summer 1972)

Solnit, Rebecca. 'On Being Grounded: Ann Hamilton Talks about the Values Informing Her Work', in *Artweek* (5 April 1989): 20

Spero, Nancy. 'Tracing Ana Mendieta', in *Artforum* (April 1992): 75-77

Tallman, Susan. 'Whose Art Is It Anyway?' (Louise Lawler), in *Art in America* (June 1991): 114-21

Turner, Jonathan. 'Giuliano Gori - Skeletons, Stairways and Thunderbolts', in *Art News* (January 1991): 75-78

Van Bruggen, Coosje. 'Bruce Nauman: Entrance, Entrapment, Exit', in *Artforum* (Summer 1986): 88-98

Verzotti, Giorgio. 'Doppel Jeopardy', in *Artforum* (November 1990): 124-29

Villaespesa, Mar. 'History's Broken Toys' (Francesc Torres), in *Artforum* (January 1991): 109-15

Vogel, Sabine. 'In Record Time' (Christian Marclay), in *Artforum* (May 1991): 103-107

Weil, Benjamin. 'Remarks on Installations and Changes in Time Dimensions', in *Flash Art* (January/February 1992): 104-109

LIST OF ILLUSTRATIONS

Half-title and p. 4
Loren Madsen
Knots
1988-90
Installation of 208 pieces of
purpleheart wood, varying sizes
17.14 x 97.53 x 36.57 m (5 ft 7 in x
32 ft x 12 ft)
Installation view, February 1990
COURTESY: DAVID MCKEE INC., NEW YORK
PHOTOGRAPH: SARAH WELLS

Title page
Ange Leccia
Arrangement
1990
COURTESY: GALLERIA CASOLI, MILAN
PHOTOGRAPH: SALVATORE LICITRA

p. 10
Marcel Duchamp
Porte, 11, Rue Larrey
1927
220 x 62.7 cm (89 x 24½ in)
COLLECTION MARY SISLER, NEW YORK

p. 11
Marcel Duchamp
Bicycle Wheel
1951; third version after lost original
of 1913
Readymade: bicycle wheel mounted
on painted wooden stool
128.27 x 64.77 x 41.91 cm (50½ x
25½ x 16 ⅝ in)
COURTESY: THE MUSEUM OF MODERN ART,
NEW YORK; THE SIDNEY AND HARRIET JANIS
COLLECTION

p. 12
Lucio Fontana
Spatial Concept (Attese)
1951
Oil on canvas
100 x 84 cm (39 ⅜ x 33 ⅛ in)

p. 15
Lyonel Feininger
Cathedral
(Bauhaus Programme)
1919
Woodcut
30.4 x 19 cm (12 x 7½ in)
COURTESY: THE MUSEUM OF MODERN ART,
NEW YORK; GIFT OF ABBY ALDRICH
ROCKEFELLER

p. 16 (above)
F. T. Marinetti
Words-in-Freedom (Irredentissimo)
c. 1912
Ink on paper
31 x 21 cm (12 x 8¼ in)
PRIVATE COLLECTION

p. 16 (below)
Vladimir Tatlin
Model for a Monument to the Third
International, Moscow
1919-20

p. 17 (above right)
Umberto Boccione
The Street Enters the House
1911
COLLECTION NIEDERSARCHSISCHE
LANDESGALERIE, HANOVER

p. 17 (below)
El Lissitzky
Proun room, November Group's Art
Exhibition, Berlin
1923
Lithograph from the first Kestner
portfolio

p. 19
Kurt Schwitters
Merzbau
c. 1925
Destroyed

p. 20 (above)
Piero Manzoni making *The Artist's
Breath*, 1961

p. 20 (below)
Marcel Duchamp
Air de Paris
1919
Readymade: glass bottle of 50 cc,
height 13.3 cm (5¼ in)
COLLECTION LOUISE AND WALTER
ARENSBERG, PHILADELPHIA MUSEUM OF ART

p. 21 (above)
First exhibition of Yves Klein's
Anthropometries of the Blue Period, 9
March 1960

p. 21 (below)
Daniel Spoerri
Dinner by Dorothy Prodber

1964
Mixed media
54.61 x 63.5 x 28 cm (21 ⅜ x 25 ⅛ x
10 ⅞ in)
COLLECTION MUSEUM OF CONTEMPORARY
ART, CHICAGO; GIFT OF MRS ROBERT B.
MAYER

p. 22
Donald Judd
From left: *Untitled*, 1991 (# 21709),
Untitled, 1991 (# 21710), *Untitled*, (#
21708), *Untitled*, 1991 (# 21707)
COURTESY: THE PACE GALLERY, NEW YORK

p. 23
Robert Morris
Observatory
1971
Santpoort-Velsen, The Netherlands

p. 24 (top)
Allan Kaprow
Yard
1961
Happening

p. 24 (centre)
Claes Oldenburg
The Store
1965
Environment

p. 24 (bottom)
Jim Dine
Car Crash (detail)
1960
Action

p. 25 (top left)
Robert Rauschenberg
Charlene
1954
Combine painting
226 x 284.5 cm (89 x 112 in)
COURTESY: STEDELIJK MUSEUM,
AMSTERDAM

p. 25 (top right)
Ed Kienholz
Roxy's
1961
Mixed media
COURTESY: LOS ANGELES COUNTY
MUSEUM OF ART; EDWARD KIENHOLZ
COLLECTION

p. 25 (centre)
Jannis Kounellis
Cavalli (Horses)
1969-76
COURTESY: GALLERIA L'ATTICO, ROME

p. 25 (bottom)
Michelangelo Pistoletto
Venus degli Stracci (Venus of the
Rags)
1967
Installed in the Galleria Gian Enzo
Sperone, Turin
COLLECTION: DI BENNARDO, NAPLES

p. 28
Susan Hiller
An Entertainment
1990
COURTESY: MATT'S GALLERY, LONDON
PHOTOGRAPH: EDWARD WOODMAN

p. 30 (above)
Robert Smithson
Installation view from the Entropic
Landscape exhibition
1993
IVAM, Valencia

p. 30 (below)
Gordon Matta-Clark
Conical Intersect
1975

p. 31
Marcel Broodthaers
La Salle Blanche
1975
39 x 457 x 600 cm (15½ x 180 x 236¼)
COURTESY: MARIA GILISSEN
PHOTOGRAPH: MARIA GILISSEN

pp. 36-37 (main picture)
Christo
The Umbrellas Japan-USA 1984-91
1991
Each umbrella 6 x 9 m (19 ft 6 in x 28
ft 9 in)
California, USA Site
PHOTOGRAPH: WOLFGANG VOLZ
COPYRIGHT: CHRISTO 1991

p. 36 (below)
Christo
The Umbrellas Japan-USA 1984-91
1991

p. 100
Barbara Kruger
Untitled
Mixed media
1991
COURTESY: MARY BOONE GALLERY, NEW YORK
PHOTOGRAPH: ZINDMAN/FREEMONT

p. 101 (above)
Cary Leibowitz ('Candyass')
Bric-a-Brac
1990
Mixed media
COURTESY: STUX GALLERY, NEW YORK

p. 101 (below)
Jenny Holzer
Under a Rock
1986-89
LED (light emitting diode) screens, black granite benches
COURTESY: INSTITUTE OF CONTEMPORARY ARTS, LONDON

p. 102 (above)
Antoni Miralda
The Wedding Cake
(From the *Honeymoon Project* 1986-92)
1989
Installed in Paris
PHOTOGRAPH: PASCAL VICTOR/ENGUERAND

p. 102 (below)
Antoni Miralda
The Eternity Ring
(From the *Honeymoon Project* 1986-92)
1991
COURTESY: IKON GALLERY, BIRMINGHAM
PHOTOGRAPH: MICHAEL WALTERS

p. 103
Station House Opera
The Bastille Dances
1989
Performance incorporating the building of a structure from concrete breeze blocks
Installed/performed in Cherbourg, France
COURTESY: THE ARTISTS
PHOTOGRAPH: BOB VAN DANTZIG

p. 104 (top and centre)
Hotel Pro Forma
Fact-Arte-Fact
1991
Performance installation
COURTESY: ROYAL MUSEUM OF FINE ART, COPENHAGEN

p. 104 (bottom)
Eleanor Antin
Loves of a Ballerina
1986
Filmic installation
COURTESY: RONALD FELDMAN GALLERY, NEW YORK
PHOTOGRAPH: D. JAMES DEE

p. 105 (above)
Matthew Barney
Field Dressing or *Transexualis*
1991
Dimensions variable
Action installation with video, sculpture and sports-related artefacts
COURTESY: STUART REGEN GALLERY, LOS ANGELES
PHOTOGRAPH: SUSAN EINSTEIN

p. 105 (below)
Shin Egashira
Male and Female on the Bed Looking at the Window
(1991 Venice Biennale of Architecture)
1991
Mixed media
Remade at the Camden Arts Centre, London

p. 106 (above)
Cildo Meirelles
Massao (missoes) (How to Build Cathedrals)
1987
Each stone 50 x 50 x 5 cm (19½ x 19½ x 2 in)
COURTESY: INSTITUTE OF CONTEMPORARY ARTS, LONDON

p. 106 (below)
Ann Hamilton
Offerings
(1991 Carnegie International)
1991
Steel, glass, melting wax, canaries
Dimensions variable
COURTESY: LOUVER GALLERY, NEW YORK
PHOTOGRAPH: MICHAEL OLIJNYK

p. 107 (above)
Aimee Morgana
Room for Hope
a. Reality Test (headboard)
b. Wishful Thinking (pillow)
c. Security Blanket (quilt)
1991
Mixed media with sound
Installed at the Pat Hearn Gallery, New York
COURTESY: AMERICAN FINE ARTS, CO.
PHOTOGRAPH: TOM WARREN

p. 107 (below)
Louise Bourgeois
Cell (Arch of Hysteria)
(From the series *Cells*)
(1993 Venice Biennale)
1989-93

p. 108 (left, above)
Genevieve Cadieux
La Felûre, au choeur des corps
(Fracture in the Chorus of the Bodies)
(1990 Venice Biennale)
1990
22 photographic panels - 6 x 13 m (19 ft 6 in x 42 ft 6 in) each
PHOTOGRAPH: CLAUDIO FRANZINI

p. 108 (left, below)
Damien Hirst
In & Out of Love
1991
Mixed media
COURTESY: TAMARA CHODZCO GALLERY, LONDON
PHOTOGRAPH: EDWARD WOODMAN

p. 108 (right)
Lucia Nogueira
Untitled
1988
COURTESY: UNIT 7 GALLERY, LONDON
PHOTOGRAPH: MINA

p. 109
Tunga
Lizart
1989
Copper, iron, lead
COURTESY: WHITECHAPEL ART GALLERY, LONDON

p. 110 (above)
Judith Barry
In the Shadow of the City...Vamp RY
1991
Slide projections
COURTESY: INSTITUTE OF CONTEMPORARY ARTS, LONDON

p. 110 (below)
Roger Welch
Drive In: Second Feature
1982

Film and sculpture installation
COURTESY: WHITNEY MUSEUM OF ART, NEW YORK

p. 111
Raimund Kummer
Wild Card
1984
Photograph, Steinway piano, sound
Installed at the Goethe House, New York

p. 112 (above)
Jonathan Borofsky
Heart Light
Light of Consciousness
1990-91
Metal and red glass sculptures, sound, paintings of the light spectrum, flyers
COURTESY: GALERIE YVON LAMBERT, PARIS
PHOTOGRAPH: KONSTANTINOS IGNATIADIS

p. 112 (below)
James Coleman
Charon (the M.I.T. Project)
1989
Slide projection with recorded narration
21 minutes
COURTESY: LISSON GALLERY, LONDON

p. 113
Alfredo Jaar
The Way It Was
('Heimat' exhibition)
1990-91
Lightboxes, photos 1 x 1.50 m (3 ft 3 in x 4 ft 11 in)
Installed at Galerie Vier, East Berlin
COURTESY: WEWERKA & WEISS GALERIE, BERLIN
PHOTOGRAPH: OLE SCHMIDT

p. 114 (left)
Rebecca Horn
The Hydra-Forest/performing: Oscar Wilde
(1988 Carnegie International)
1988
Glass, mercury, electric chandelier
COURTESY: CARNEGIE MUSEUM OF ART, PITTSBURGH

p. 114 (right, below)
Angela Bulloch
Untitled
1989
Spherical lights
Installed at Castella di Rivoli, Turin
(organized by Franz Paludetto,

curated by Kate MacFarlane)
COURTESY: PALEY WRIGHT INTERIM ART LTD.

p. 115 (above)
Sarkis
Elle danse dans l'atelier de Sarkis avec le quatuor No 15 de Dimitri Shostakovich (She danced around Sarkis' studio to the Dimitri Shostakovich quartet No 15)
('Heimat' exhibition)
1990
Video installation with mixed media
COURTESY: WEWERKA & WEISS GALERIE, BERLIN
PHOTOGRAPH: L. D. HASLAM

p. 115 (below)
Marianne Berenhaut
Vie privée (Private Life)
1989
Mixed media
Installed at La Gare du Watermael, Brussels
COURTESY: THE ARTIST
PHOTOGRAPH: JACQUES SIMON

p. 116 (above)
Keith Sonnier
Tetrapod Wall
1988
Neon, glass, aluminium
2.74 x 2.46 x 2.27 m (108 x 97 x 89 ft)
COURTESY: LEO CASTELLI GALLERY, NEW YORK
PHOTOGRAPH: STEVEN TUCKER

p. 116 (below)
Alfredo Pirri
Gas
1990
Light, oil on canvas, chalky coloured pigment, metal
Metal structure 310 x 150 x 125 cm (122 x 59 x 49¼ in), with 18 elements of 310 x 30 x 5 cm (122 x 11 ¾ x 2 in). The word GAS on wall 110 x 110 cm (43¼ x 43¼ inches)
COURTESY: GALLERIA TUCCI RUSSO, TURIN
PHOTOGRAPH: ENZO RICCI

p. 117 (above)
Dan Flavin
'Monument' for V. Tatlin
1969, 1970; 1991
Cool white fluorescent light
Each light sculpture 244 x 81 x 11 cm (96 x 32 x 4½ in)
COURTESY: MARY BOONE GALLERY, NEW YORK 1991

PHOTOGRAPH: ZINDMAN/FREMONT, NEW YORK

p. 117 (below)
Andrew Greaves
Look at, walk through, and listen to
1991
COURTESY: THE ARTIST AND THE MUSEUM OF INSTALLATION, LONDON
PHOTOGRAPH: EDWARD WOODMAN

p. 118
Bill Culbert
An Explanation of Light: The Serpentine Windows
1983
Fluorescent light
Installed at the Serpentine Gallery, London
COURTESY: VICTORIA MIRO GALLERY, LONDON

p. 119 (left)
Bill Culbert
Untitled
(1990 Tyneside International Exhibition)
Fluorescent light
1990

p. 119 (right)
Bruce Nauman
Changing Light Corridor with Rooms
1972/1988
Wood and fluorescent lights
Corridor: 3 x 0.8 x 12.2 m (10 x 2 x 40 ft)
Rectangular room: 6 x 3 m (20 x 10 ft)
Triangular room: 7 x 4.6 x 4.6 m (23 x 15 x 15 ft)
COURTESY: ANTHONY D'OFFAY GALLERY, LONDON

p. 120 (top and centre)
Cornelia Parker
Cold Dark Matter - An Exploded View
1991
Garden shed and contents
COURTESY: CHISENHALE GALLERY, LONDON

p. 120 (bottom)
John Coleman
Lapwing Redwing Fieldfare
1992
COURTESY: MUSEUM OF INSTALLATION, LONDON

p. 121
Christian Boltanski

Les Ombres (The Shadows)
1986
Wooden puppets, cardboard, tin, corks, projectors, fan
Installed at Musée de Nice
COURTESY: THE ARTIST, GALERIE GHISLAINE HUSSENOT, PARIS

p. 122
Pierpaolo Calzolari
Untitled
1990
Copper, lead, refrigerating engine
168 x 231 x 98 cm (66 x 91 x 38½ in)
COURTESY: GENTILI ARTE CONTEMPORANEA, FLORENCE
PHOTOGRAPH: CARLO FEI

p. 123 (above)
Maurizio Mochetti
Quartz Spheres
1989
Laser and quartz spheres
44 spheres
COURTESY: EDWARD TOTAH GALLERY, LONDON
PHOTOGRAPH: HUGH KELLY

p. 123 (below)
Mona Hatoum
Light at the End
1989
Metal frame, heating elements
COURTESY: DAVID THORPE, THE SHOWROOM, LONDON
PHOTOGRAPH: EDWARD WOODMAN

p. 128
Barbara Bloom
The Reign of Narcissism
1990
Mixed media
First installed at the Museum of Contemporary Art, Los Angeles, in 1989
COURTESY: SERPENTINE GALLERY, LONDON

p. 129 (above)
Sharon Kivland and Ben Hillwood-Harris
The Abandonment of Origins
1990
Mixed media
9.14 x 6.09 x 2.74 m (30 x 20 x 9 ft)
Installed at Watermans Art Centre, London, 21 April-21 May 1989; Mappin Art Gallery, Sheffield, 13 October-11 November 1990
COURTESY: THE ARTISTS

p. 129 (below)
Michael Asher
Untitled
(1991 Carnegie International)
1991
Mixed media
Dimensions variable
COURTESY: THE ARTIST

p. 130 (above)
Adrian Piper
Cornered
1988
Video installation with table, lighting, birth certificate
17 minutes
COURTESY: JOHN WEBER GALLERY, NEW YORK

p. 130 (below)
Braco Dimitrijevic
The Casual Passer-By I Met
1988
Photograph
COURTESY: THE HAYWARD GALLERY, LONDON
PHOTOGRAPH: EDWARD WOODMAN

p. 131 (above)
Tim Head
The Tyranny of Reason
1985
Slide projections, mirrors, barbed wire, sound
Installed at the Institute of Contemporary Arts, London
COURTESY: THE ARTIST
PHOTOGRAPH: CHRIS DAVIES

p. 131 (below)
David Ireland
Repository
1988
Metal filing cabinet, folders, chicken wire
COURTESY: UNIVERSITY ART MUSEUM, UNIVERSITY OF CALIFORNIA, BERKELEY

p. 132 (above, left and right)
Louise Sudell
Second Skin
1992
White sheeting, snakeskins, facial peels, wigs made from the artist's hair
Installed in a disused building, previously the Archive for Foreign Affairs, The Hague

p. 132 (below), p. 133 (below)
Robert Gober

INDEX